THE
LINCOLN CENTER
STORY

THE LINCOLN CENTER STORY

by Alan Rich

AMERICAN HERITAGE • New York

Distributed by Houghton Mifflin Company • Boston

Library of Congress Cataloging in Publication Data

Rich, Alan.
    The Lincoln Center story.

    1. Lincoln Center for the Performing Arts. I. Title.
PN1588.N5R5 1984   790.2′09747′1   84-6441
ISBN 0-8281-1169-3

Printed in the United States of America

Table of Contents

Above: Beverly Sills accepts confetti, balloons, streamers, and thunderous applause after her gala farewell performance at the New York State Theater, October 27, 1980. Half-title page: Jacques Lipchitz's bronze relief "Birth of the Muses" hangs in the lobby of the State Theater. Title page: The New York Philharmonic plays to a full house at Avery Fisher Hall.

Introduction

The fountain at the center of the plaza of Lincoln Center is a beautiful sight and a wonderful gathering place, but to me it is more than just a gloriously bubbling show of water. Faced by three great halls and surrounded by the others behind them, it represents the heart of Lincoln Center —the intermingling of great creative energies, the constant celebration of all the creative arts that flourish together at Lincoln Center. The fourteen acres surrounding the fountain are alive with activity all day and evening all year long. During daytime, rehearsals are conducted, sets are built, teaching in the performing arts takes place at the Juilliard School and throughout the Center, tours are conducted, stages are prepared, future events are planned, scholars and enthusiasts study or browse at the performing-arts library, afternoon events such as outdoor performances are held, people arrive to buy tickets, to picnic, or just to enjoy the ambience. Toward evening, the crowds begin to grow. The Center's cafés begin serving pretheater meals, and neighborhood restaurants fill with early diners. The plaza becomes aswarm with people as the halls open their doors for

The orchestra in the pit tunes its instruments and the audience takes its seats before a performance of Giacomo Meyerbeer's enormous opera Le Prophète, *at the Metropolitan Opera House in 1977.*

the evening events, and people from all over New York, the nation, and the world prepare to enjoy the productions of several of our most prestigious and best-loved cultural institutions.

The performances themselves cover a staggering range. Two leading opera companies, the Metropolitan and the New York City Opera, perform numerous operas within each week of their seasons; the Philharmonic gives more than 130 orchestral concerts in Avery Fisher Hall each year; the New York City Ballet presents about forty-five different productions during each nine-week stint; the Chamber Music Society and the Mostly Mozart Festival provide extensive programs of music for smaller ensembles; the Film Society of Lincoln Center adds motion pictures to the fare; the Bruno Walter Auditorium at the public library allows up-and-coming artists to give free recitals; the Vivian Beaumont and Mitzi E. Newhouse theaters can play host to major stage productions; on top of all that, distinguished artists and performing groups of every kind from all over the world fill the halls when they might otherwise be dark. What all these performers and performances have in common is a sharing of excellence; what they add up to is an almost never-ending festival of the performing arts at their best, all in one unifying location, around that fountain.

No single book could possibly convey everything that goes on at Lincoln Center. This book, however, gives a excellent short history of the Center to commemorate the twenty-fifth anniversary of its groundbreaking in 1959. Lincoln Center began as a vision—a vision of performing and educational institutions drawn together in a common environment and working among themselves in a spirit of creative partnership. They would share a dedication to the highest quality in the arts and to public service. This vision was nurtured in the minds of several men, John D. Rockefeller 3rd and Robert Moses prominent among them. It was a novel and adventurous idea—as hard as it is to imagine today, no such ambitious performing-arts center then existed anywhere. And it proved to be a constantly challenging undertaking, involving the winning of popular support, the assemblage of land, the construction of worthy buildings, and, possibly most difficult of all, the wooing of great, independent cultural enterprises to come share the same ground.

Fortunately, each of the original constituent organizations has remained as strong and independent as ever since coming to Lincoln Center. As few could have predicted, each has in fact benefited from its association with the Center, and their presence together in this one place has helped create an environ-

ment where new programs, such as the Lincoln Center Institute, the Mostly Mozart Festival, Great Performers, the Out-of-Doors series, the Chamber Music Society, and the Film Society, could thrive, widening the Center's artistic scope and appeal even further. With each new program, the Center has grown to take on a major artistic identity and life of its own, yet miraculously this has only served to add to, not detract from, the health and prominence of each of its constituent organizations.

The Lincoln Center story is exciting because it is a success story about people coming together out of love for the performing arts. Yet there is more to the Center than even that suggests. Lincoln Center has not only helped the arts, it has played an important constructive role in the life of the city. First and foremost, of course, it has helped build the local audience for the arts. Also, the Center has helped crystallize the city's role as a world center for the performing arts. Additionally, it has created jobs and tourism and has helped spur the revival of a whole section of town— the Upper West Side of Manhattan. Lincoln Center has proved to be a valuable investment in the economy, as well as the spirit, of New York City.

Yet the stewards of Lincoln Center have never felt it sufficient to look out only as far as the city, so we always take great pleasure in the trips that the Lincoln Center companies take, bringing live cultural excitement to cities all over the United States and the world. And we're especially proud of our many radio and television broadcasts. "Live From Lincoln Center" (and a year later, "Live From the Met", first shown on nationwide public television in 1976, has brought Lincoln Center into the homes of as many as 100 million Americans.

The performing arts by their very nature depend on healthy communication between performers and their audience, so we continue to reach out in every way we can, making every effort to serve an even greater audience. At the same time, we have tried to nurture the Center as a place for artists and scholars and others to come to from all over the world, a place both to share one's talents and to learn. The Juilliard School is now generally regarded as the foremost institution in the world for the training of professionals in music, opera, dance, and drama. The Lincoln Center Institute, founded in 1974, now reaches 80,000 young people a year with live performances at their schools and at the Center, and it offers intensive programs each summer to hundreds of teachers from New York, New Jersey, and Connecticut. In addition, each constituent organization has its own more specialized educational program.

When we think of the success of Lincoln Center,

we think first of the talent, inspiration, and hard work of its performing artists and the many other people who labor here, but their efforts would not be possible without a steady underpinning of generous financial help from many sources. Individuals, foundations, federal, state, and city governments, and corporations donate millions of dollars every year; without them there could be no Lincoln Center. Ticket sales cover as much of our costs as they reasonably can—it is our responsibility to remain as affordable as possible yet not to compromise on artistic standards, so we must depend on a wide variety of support. To meet our tremendous needs, we have been fortunate in developing new forms of funding, including a Lincoln Center Consolidated Corporate Fund that contributes to each of the constituent organizations, helping to provide what their own fund drives cannot. Corporations have played a bigger and bigger part in assisting the arts in recent years, and today's leaders of big business understand better than ever how serving the arts can mean serving not just culture but also the city, the nation, related industries, and, ultimately, whatever business is doing the giving. Hundreds of individuals know how much we depend on their help, too, and the Chairman's Council serves to encourage and thank those who are able to give substantial annual donations. The Lincoln Center Fund, an endowment drive for the entire center, has just passed the $25 million mark. It is especially valuable for the support it gives to Lincoln Center's various community programs, including free outdoor concerts and the annual holiday festival.

The firm organizational and financial foundation for Lincoln Center was laid by many people. Foremost among them was the late John D. Rockefeller 3rd, who, leading a visionary committee, ably perceived the possibilities for Lincoln Center and consistently found ways of realizing them. His work has been built upon and strengthened by hundreds, if not thousands, of others who have given time, energy, and inspiration to this grand adventure. A list of the names of past and present officers of Lincoln Center, Inc., and its constituent organizations, on pages 126 and 127, gives but a small idea of the many who have helped, and each name can only suggest a battery of others whose labors have also been most valuable. I wish I could thank everyone here; that is not possible, but I know that the many people of Lincoln Center have been recognized in many ways over the years, and Lincoln Center represents a testimony to their efforts as well as a home to the arts it and they have served. I would like, however, to single out two people for special personal thanks—William Schuman, president of Lincoln Center from 1962 to 1969, and

Amyas Ames, my predecessor as chairman of Lincoln Center, Inc. I thank Bill Schuman for bringing me into the active life of Lincoln Center in 1967/68 to participate, with William F. May, in the creation of the Film Society and for inspiring my joy in all of Lincoln Center's efforts. I am also most appreciative of Amyas Ames's friendship and special leadership for eleven years, from 1970 until 1981. During that period, Lincoln Center grew from a youthful enterprise into a solidly established institution. Above all, I'm grateful to the board of directors and staff of Lincoln Center, Inc., whose hard, effective work is enabling our best hopes and plans to become reality right now.

This book tells about Lincoln Center's past and present; our job is to think about its present and future. Fortunately, we see the future as full of opportunity, and we are optimistic and excited about it. We perceive our job as twofold: to help maintain the excellence that Lincoln Center has come to signify and to help expand that excellence and bring new ideas to fruition. Perhaps the most important recent development for the performing arts everywhere is their rapidly increasing proliferation through radio, television, and other media. Lincoln Center is proud to have been in the vanguard in making this happen, developing new techniques for effective live broadcasting and reaching unprecedented audiences with the results. We will continue to do all we can to help lead the way.

We also see a great opportunity for helping to build the audiences of tomorrow. Many of our educational programs are designed toward that end; in the future we hope especially to do more to bring the performing arts to children. We know we can communicate the joy of the arts to the young and can encourage the unleashing of their creative energy. The arts can and should enrich the lives of everybody, and it is Lincoln Center's aim to try to bring them to everybody.

John D. Rockefeller 3rd, perhaps the most important single figure in the history of Lincoln Center, said words in 1963 that have been a sort of banner for the Center ever since. He said, "The arts are not for the privileged few, but for the many. Their place is not on the periphery of daily life, but at its center."

Martin E. Segal, Chairman
Lincoln Center for the Performing Arts, Inc.
October, 1984

1
The Dream

May 14, 1959. After several days of soaking rain the sun was out over New York this morning; the day had dawned clear, bright, and, one might add, propitious. At a building site at Columbus and West Sixty-fourth, workmen put a final touch on the setting for a ceremony: a small pavilion for dignitaries, a green-striped tent big enough to hold a symphony orchestra, and thousands of folding chairs set out for invited guests. At the appointed hour of 11:00 A.M., Leonard Bernstein led the New York Philharmonic in Aaron Copland's "Fanfare for the Common Man"; then came the traditional "Hail to the Chief" as President Dwight D. Eisenhower was escorted to his seat. Lincoln Center for the Performing Arts was seeing its first audience, resounding to its first music. Three years and some months would pass before the doors would open at an actual building on that acreage; on this day it showed only mud and rubble. Someone else would be living in the White House before the promises in the president's speech that morning would start to be fulfilled —promises of a "great cultural adventure," a "mighty influence for peace and under-

Lincoln Center glows in the evening. The three large buildings surrounding the plaza and fountain are, from left, the New York State Theater, the Metropolitan Opera House, and Avery Fisher Hall.

This block now holds the main plaza and the Met.

Eisenhower lifts the first shovel.

Twelve thousand people atte

This 1955 aerial view of Manhattan, looking southeast, shows the future site of Lincoln Center outlined in white.

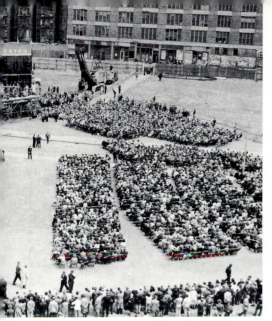

ground-breaking ceremony, May 14, 1959.

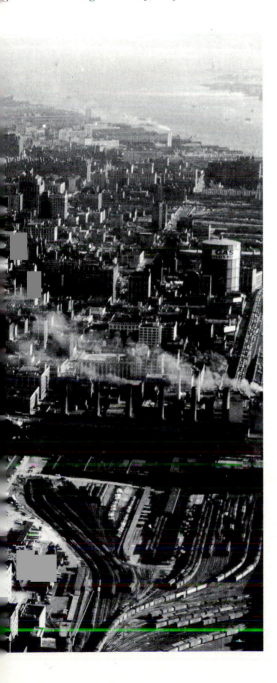

standing throughout the world." But now there was a beginning; it happened when Dwight Eisenhower bent over to break Lincoln Center's ground with a ceremonial shovel. He held on to that shovelful of New York's earth until the photographers had snapped their fill; then the Philharmonic and the Juilliard Chorus lit into Handel's "Hallelujah" chorus, and the artistic life of New York City—and of the world—rounded a corner and moved into a new era.

Where does one start the story of Lincoln Center? It goes back, surely, four years before that ground-breaking, to a time when city authorities tagged the sprawl of decaying tenements around Manhattan's Lincoln Square as ripe for demolition and urban renewal, and when, at the same moment, some of New York's top leaders in the performing arts happened to be emerging from their present antiquated facilities and searching for new homes. In a way, the great Lincoln Center story owes its start to a matter of the right need at the right time.

New York's existence as a center for the arts had always been ridden by need. On May 20, 1846, the four-year-old New York Philharmonic put on a benefit concert at Castle Garden, in the Battery; the purpose was to raise money to build "Philharmonic Hall," a permanent home for the orchestra. It was a gala event, the first American performance of Beethoven's Ninth Symphony. The attendance numbered 2,000 and the net was the hardly princely sum of $390. The orchestra went on to make its home in a series of rented halls for another 116 years before it finally got a Philharmonic Hall to call its own.

In 1955 the Metropolitan Opera also needed a new home; its old auditorium just below Times Square was beautiful enough to pass for an opera house, but the performing amenities there had disintegrated beyond redemption. Yet that same building had represented the triumphant fulfillment of a need back in the 1880s: the need of New York's social aristocracy—the Vanderbilt family most of all—for an opera house with enough box seats to assure its patrons the same place of honor year after year. By 1955, however, the gold paint on those loges had begun to peel. Mid-Manhattan commercial interests had grown up around Thirty-ninth and Broadway, further eroding the grandeur that should be the Metropolitan Opera's birthright. There was no storage space for scenery; last night's opera had to be pushed out onto the sidewalk to await being trucked away. And General Manager Rudolf Bing's hope of restoring opera

The Met's home on Fourteenth Street, the 1854 Academy of Music (above), contained only eighteen boxes.

The old Metropolitan Opera House (opposite), at Broadway and Thirty-ninth Street, was the company's home from 1883 to 1966.

as a dramatic experience as well as a musical feast was thwarted by the large number of seats from which you could see but a tiny sliver of stage. Clearly it was time for the venerable Met to move elsewhere.

Two of Manhattan's main thoroughfares, Broadway and Columbus Avenue, meet at Lincoln Square, at about Sixty-fourth Street. In 1954 the surrounding blocks, an enclave of tenements and small stores, had deteriorated into a slum, and Robert Moses, New York's master builder who was then the city's slum clearance administrator, proposed turning them into a place for culture. Specifically, he saw a grand opera house ensconced somewhere on the property, so he approached the board of the Metropolitan Opera with his plans, bringing along his good friend the architect Wallace K. Harrison to add a foundation to his vision.

The idea of abandoning the "yellow brick brewery" (an early epithet for the house at Thirty-ninth and Broadway) for the greener pastures of uptown had long been on the Met's mind. In fact, the patch of expensive mid-Manhattan real estate known as Rockefeller Center had begun as a project to build a new home for the Met; those old unrealized plans look glamorous indeed, with a public square (located about where the skating rink is now) leading the eye toward a new hall for the most fabulous of the performing arts. Rockefeller Center's land purchase had been engineered by John D. Rockefeller, Jr., bearer of a name that was to figure prominently in the development of Lincoln Center. The architect for that planned opera house had been Wallace K. Harrison, who would later create the master plan for Lincoln Center— and would finally create the Metropolitan Opera House that stands today. The Metropolitan Opera never made the move to Fiftieth Street and Sixth Avenue. Its financial resources were too hard hit by "Black Friday," 1929, at the stock market.

Moses's original 1954 idea was for the Met to go it alone. With the world's grandest grand opera installed at Lincoln Square, how much more culture could that neighborhood absorb? But New York's other great musical institution was in even worse straits at the time. The owners of Carnegie Hall, where the Philharmonic had been the principal tenant since the turn of the century, announced that their hall—beloved by generations of musicians and music-lovers, its name at the time synonymous with excellence in the concert-giving world, but a money-loser nonetheless— would be demolished in 1959, at the termination of the Philharmonic's lease. It suddenly made sense to all concerned

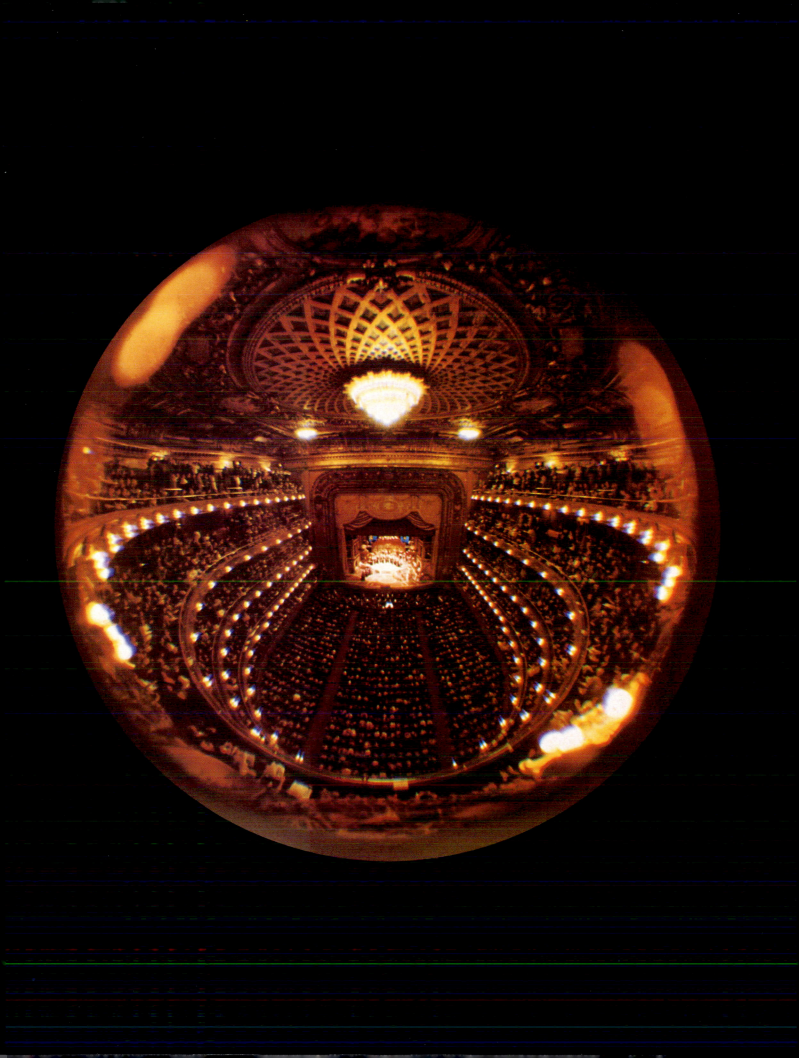

The old Met had poor sightlines from the upper balconies (above and right), inadequate backstage facilities, and almost no storage space at all, so sets had to be trucked off after each performance (below).

with the Lincoln Square idea to include a home for the orchestra in the new plans. The Philharmonic's management had already approached Wallace Harrison for advice on planning a new home; Harrison now became the catalyst that brought the orchestra's board into the discussions for the Lincoln Square project.

The idea was startling, to say the least, as if Macy's had gone into partnership with Gimbels; New York's two musical monoliths, rivals not in repertory but rivals certainly for the ticket-buyer's and patron's dollars, forming some sort of real-estate alliance. Where would it all lead?

The answer came soon enough. Early building estimates—they make amusing reading today—came to $15 million for a new Met and $5 million for Philharmonic Hall. Throughout the summer of 1955, the Metropolitan Opera and the New York Philharmonic applied themselves to beating bushes for money for their new buildings, and occasionally they found themselves beating the same bush at the same time. Meanwhile, New York's cultural leadership gradually perceived that something even grander than a two-party Met-Philharmonic entente might possibly be in order. Such a thought occurred to Robert Moses and to several Metropolitan Opera board members as well: why not a full-scale center for the arts, with several buildings and a consortium of performing organizations, all linked in a corporate identity that might become a more potent fund-raising force than any single constituent?

There was no specific moment in history when a couple of building plans for some cleared land at Lincoln Square became transformed into Lincoln Center for the Performing Arts, but suddenly that was the bright star on the horizon. In September 1955 Charles M. Spofford, chairman of the Metropolitan Opera's executive committee, happened to find himself at an out-of-town conference with John D. Rockefeller 3rd, chairman of the Rockefeller Foundation and member of a family whose patronage of the arts forms a noble chapter in American cultural annals. The two men discussed the concept of an all-embracing center for the arts. Later, Rockefeller wrote of that meeting, "For me new horizons began to open."

Today, a quarter of a century after the sun-drenched ground-breaking at Lincoln Center, the idea of an arts center, of a physical bringing together of every diverse element in the realm of performance under one roof or on one plot of land, seems perfectly normal; it's a way of cultural life in many cities around the world. Washington has its Kennedy Center, Los Angeles its Music Center, London its South Bank —all inspired by the Lincoln Center example. But back in 1955, none of those places had been built. You'd have had to run the clock back to a Medici palace in Renaissance Florence to find the kind of complex of culture that had now seized the imaginations of six pioneering men in New York.

The six were the exploratory team of Charles M. Spofford and Anthony A. Bliss of the Metropolitan Opera's executive committee; Floyd Blair and Arthur A. Houghton, Jr., of the New York Philharmonic-Symphony Society; the architect Wallace K. Harrison; and John D. Rockefeller 3rd. Over a series of working lunches they held beginning on

The house on Thirty-ninth Street was beloved by opera-goers; however, its unspectacular exterior caused it to be popularly nicknamed "the yellow brick brewery."

17

The Academy of Music

The Apollo Rooms (Euterpian Hall)

Castle Garden

Above are five of the places where the Philharmonic resided in the 120 years before its Lincoln Center hall opened. All except Carnegie Hall were on Fourteenth Street or below; none was a permanent home.

October 25, 1955, the outlines of the center became sketched in with ever clearer strokes. By the year's end, and with several members added to the committee, Spofford was able to define its mission: "...to determine the feasibility of a musical arts center in the City not only for the opera and symphony but also for such activities as chamber music, ballet, light opera, and spoken drama, and possible educational programs related thereto [and to determine] the facilities that would be required, and the best methods of financing such a project." The outlines of what we know as Lincoln Center are clearly discernible in these words.

From the beginning, doubts were raised, at first among the committee members and later in the press and by the man on the street. What kind of daring scheme was this, gathering together New York's most prestigious artistic assets into some kind of cultural supermarket? Why, of all places, at this rubble-strewn site on Columbus in the West Sixties, served by only a single nearby subway, with few if any decent restaurants, and beset by a traffic bottleneck

Niblo's Garden

Carnegie Hall

where heavy trucks veered off Broadway to plunge down-town along Columbus Avenue? What about parking? What about all that traffic and subway noise, which would certainly resound inside the buildings themselves as it often does at Carnegie Hall? What about the impact on the rest of the city, if local cultural organizations abandoned their neighborhood followings and headed for the Lincoln Center big time?

As we now know, few if any of these negative projections or fears came to pass. The flow of traffic past Lincoln Center, still an obstacle for the late concertgoer, is no worse than anywhere else in mid-Manhattan, and the architects and sound engineers wrought wonders in soundproofing Lincoln Center from the roar of the real world only a few yards distant. Nor is the parking situation worse than New York City's norm. Whatever hurdles lay in the paths of the planners and builders of Lincoln Center, at least these phantoms never materialized.

There were, and would long be, real dangers. As the

Leopold Stokowski

Sir John Barbirolli

Bruno Walter

Most of this century's greatest conductors have led the Philharmonic. Arturo Toscanini (shown below with the orchestra at Carnegie Hall) was principal conductor from 1928 through 1936; the six pictured above were also associated with the orchestra.

concept of an all-embracing arts center expanded from one committee lunch to the next, so did the need for land for the buildings. It wouldn't be easy to attain. The wily Moses had a few ideas for the rest of the surrounding bulldozed vacant land; for instance, a project was under discussion to develop a commercial theatrical district, under the leadership of the noted theater impresario Roger L. Stevens, at the outskirts of the original Lincoln Center territory. That would have placed a theater just about where the box office of Avery Fisher Hall is now located. Some persuasive words from Rockefeller, however, induced Moses to roll Lincoln Center's

George Szell *Walter Damrosch* *Dimitri Mitropoulos*

boundary northward from Sixty-fourth Street to Sixty-fifth, and when later on the plans for Stevens's theatrical complex fell apart, another half-block, on the north side of Sixty-fifth Street, was added to the Lincoln Center stakeout. That became the site of the building now shared by the Juilliard School and Alice Tully Hall.

On June 22, 1956, the secretary of state's office in Albany issued a certificate of incorporation to The Lincoln Center for the Performing Arts, Inc., as a nonprofit institution "to sustain and encourage the musical and performing arts." The corporation was authorized to own real estate

Robert Moses (left) and General Maxwell Taylor, president of Lincoln Center, Inc. sign a memorandum of understanding for the New York World's Fair.

within its allotted demesne and "to encourage, sponsor, or facilitate performances and exhibitions, to commission the creation of new works, and voluntarily assist the education of artists and students of these arts."

A noble premise that, and one that fairly teems with significance. The concept of a Lincoln Center organization may have begun with landlordly considerations: purchase of land, maintenance of buildings, sweeping of leaves off walkways and out of fountains. Now there was a mandate along vastly different lines. No longer just a proprietor, Lincoln Center had achieved an identity as a cultural force in and of itself, responsible for bringing into the world not only buildings and fountains but works of living art: plays, operas, symphonies. The constituents of the city's artistic life that would someday be gathered at Lincoln Center would find in this new organization a potent friend—and sometimes an artistic rival as well.

Three years from incorporation to ground-breaking: it seems a long time, but there was work to be done. Lincoln Center had its mandate; it now faced two crushing problems: assembling a full list of constituents—the cultural organizations that would become part of the Center—and planning the buildings to house and placate these artistic factions that would soon come together at the doorstep. Neither proved easy.

The tentative list of constituents called for the Met, the Philharmonic, a nonprofit repertory theatrical troupe, and the Juilliard School of Music, each to inhabit its own building erected with private funds; a ballet company would move into a theater to be built by New York State for the

The officers and board of directors of Lincoln

Center, Inc., hold a meeting in the early 1960s. John D. Rockefeller 3rd is at left, his hand upraised.

1964/65 New York World's Fair and then turned over to the city; and a city-financed Library & Museum of the Performing Arts would house the incomparable research holdings of the New York Public Library hitherto crammed into several branches. To design the homes for this distinguished roster, an equally distinguished group of architects was summoned: Harrison for the Met and as overall design coordinator; Max Abramovitz for Philharmonic Hall; Philip Johnson for the New York State Theater (as the ballet theater came to be

Above, four early sketches of Lincoln Center suggest the evolution of architects' plans. The first view (from left to right), from 1957, shows the three central buildings placed around a fountain, but with none of the final details worked out. In the second view, from 1958, the Metropolitan Opera House has been pulled closer in and the Julliard area has been added. By 1959, the theater next to the Met begins to take shape; in 1960, the Center looks almost as it does today—except that an Opera Tower, later abandoned, rises behind the Metropolitan Opera House.

called); Gordon Bunshaft for the Library-Museum; Eero Saarinen, chosen with the approval of Mrs. Vivian Beaumont Allen for the repertory theater that would bear her (maiden) name; Pietro Belluschi for the building that would house Juilliard and the chamber music hall generously contributed by and named for Alice Tully.

These were the buildings and what they would offer. The exact occupancy of the ballet theater was, however, in doubt. The obvious choice, George Balanchine's New York City Ballet, was already attached to the New York City Center of Music and Drama, that struggling but immensely popular arts-center prototype that Mayor Fiorello H. La Guardia had hurled into life during World War II. Like the old Met, City Center's facilities were primitive, its sightlines, well, weird. But the theater was lovable and cheap to run. Neither Balanchine's New York City Ballet nor that other City Center jewel, Julius Rudel's New York City Opera, was at all sure in 1956 that it wanted to forsake the sentiment-laden old barn. But leave it they both did, and willingly,

The principal architects of Lincoln Center posed together for the photograph at left in 1958. Seated, from left to right, are Wallace K. Harrison, Philip Johnson, Eero Saarinen, and Gordon Bunshaft. Standing are Pietro Belluschi and Max Abramovitz.

when a new home at Lincoln Center became a reality.

A sheaf of original designs for Lincoln Center is as surprising today as those original cost estimates. At one time the plan called for a north-south mall from Sixty-second Street to Sixty-fifth midway through the property, with the grand buildings on either side. Eventually good psychology prevailed; with the axis of the mall rotated ninety degrees, putting the glassed-in, brightly illuminated front of Harrison's Metropolitan Opera House at its terminus, Lincoln Center could cast its beams over all of Manhattan. At one time, in fact, a mall was to have led eastward from Columbus through to Central Park. It never happened; when Lincoln Center became a reality, land in that once-blighted part of Manhattan suddenly became too precious to squander on wide-open space. It might have been wonderful, a broad avenue opening to even broader urban vistas. But for millions who have visited and enjoyed the wonders of the place, Lincoln Center has broadened horizons far beyond what any mere patch of real estate could have accomplished.

2
Family Matters

William Howard Schuman was already considered a major American composer when in 1945, at the age of thirty-five, he took over the presidency of the Juilliard School of Music. In the seventeen years that followed, he transformed the school from a place primarily concerned with teaching technique into one that cared for the mind of the musician no less than for his or her fingers. In 1957, when Juilliard became a Lincoln Center constituent, Schuman joined the Lincoln Center Council. In 1962 he was named president of Lincoln Center itself. The timing was right; before 1962 the most pressing matter at the Center had been getting the buildings up and paid for, and the Center's first president, General Maxwell D. Taylor, had accomplished wonders at that during his year in office. Now it was time to aim the spotlight on artistic matters, and that was where Schuman's authority came in. He would have to care for Lincoln Center's artistic family, the existing organizations as well as new projects still in the talking stage, and forge an identity for the whole of Lincoln Center that would still, somehow, respect the integrity of the separate

This was the view from above the stage of the Metropolitan Opera House, looking out toward the auditorium and beyond, on June 3, 1964. The hall finally opened more than two years later, on September 16, 1966.

Alexander Calder and grandson observe the installation of his stabile Le Guichet *on November 11, 1965.*

The city, including countless passersby, watched eagerly as construction of Lincoln Center progressed. At center, workers toil at Philharmonic Hall in March 1961.

constituents. It would not be easy.

When Schuman took office on January 1, 1962, Lincoln Center's visible structure consisted of little more than one almost-finished building, Philharmonic Hall. Scheduled to open in 1961, the hall was now a year behind; its budget, originally projected at $5 million, had risen to $14.2 million. The new Metropolitan Opera House was a large hole (dubbed Lake Bing for its tendency to flood); its construction budget, $37.4 million, was more than twice the $15 million first forecast. Work on the building to house the New York Public Library and the new repertory theater was due to start in September 1962. There had been no work whatever on the building for Juilliard and the chamber music hall. The $20 million New York State Theater was under way—it was scheduled to open concurrently with the World's Fair in 1964 —but it, too, had no constituent as yet.

Everybody knew, however, who that constituent would be. The theater had, after all, been conceived as a place for dance, and George Balanchine had frequently been consulted on the stage and backstage design even while his New York City Ballet seemed happily domiciled at creaky old City Center, eight blocks away. On April 1, 1963, after much

wooing and protesting on both sides, the New York City Ballet agreed to perform a twenty-week season each year at the New York State Theater. The New York City Opera joined up soon after, and in April 1965 the City Center organization agreed to assume full operating responsibility at the State Theater.

Meanwhile, Schuman had invited the great theatrical composer Richard Rodgers to organize the Music Theater of Lincoln Center, a company that would use periods of downtime at the New York State Theater for deluxe revivals of historic Broadway musicals. Schuman had some further projects as well to enhance Lincoln Center's cultural panorama. One of them, off in the future awaiting the completion of the chamber music hall, was the Chamber Music Society of Lincoln Center, a resident ensemble of world-class chamber musicians; another was the Film Society of Lincoln Center, which would start up in 1967. The latter's first president was Martin E. Segal—now chairman of the board of Lincoln Center.

This, then, was the whole family: two opera companies, a symphony orchestra, a ballet company, a theatrical troupe, a chamber music ensemble, a film society, a school for the

Julius Rudel, director from 1957 to 1979

Gianna Rolandi

Samuel Ramey

The New York State Theater

The New York City Opera, founded in 1943, made the State Theater its home beginning in 1966. Above are several of the many stars the company has produced over the years.

arts, and a performing-arts library and research facility—all on one patch of Manhattan real estate that within living memory had presented a virtual textbook study in urban decay.

As families go, it was certainly an interesting mixture—of ages, of artistic philosophies, of ways of appealing to an audience. Let's take a closer look at some of those established performance organizations, as the Lincoln Center family of the 1960s sits for its portrait.

Leonard Bernstein was in his glory as the head of the New York Philharmonic (founded in 1842, it merged with the New York Symphony in 1928 to become the Philharmonic-Symphony Society of New York but was never known as anything but "the Philharmonic"). The Philharmonic belonged then, as it always will, among America's top half-dozen orchestras. Its great conductors had included Arturo Toscanini in the 1930s and Bruno Walter. Under Bernstein's direction, the Philharmonic was in a halcyon era; the man's charismatic podium manner, his enterprising forays into hith-

Sherrill Milnes

erto unknown repertory (the Mahler symphonies, challenging new music), and his continuous high visibility—in society, in the media—were the stuff of conversation among New York's musical connoisseurs, those who admired him and those who didn't. Under Bernstein the Philharmonic had a thrilling tone, urgent and communicative.

Rudolf Bing, general manager of the Metropolitan Opera (founded in 1883), was never considered exactly charismatic, but he brought the company to an artistic level beyond anything it had recently achieved. He, too, was a seeker after new, or at least hitherto unexplored, repertory. He came to the Met in 1950 and addressed himself first to making opera a dramatic experience for the eye as well as the ear. Under him famous artists designed sets; famous directors from legitimate theater—even from films—set to work revitalizing familiar repertory and breathing life into novelties. Few could question Bing's passionate dedication to the highest artistic standards, but that passion embroiled him with the public more than once. He fired singers of huge audience

31

The City Opera has long had a reputation as a show-place for modern American works. One such is Douglas Moore's The Ballad of Baby Doe which the company brought to the State Theater in its first Lincoln Center season, in 1966.

appeal (Maria Callas, for one, along with Helen Traubel, Lauritz Melchior, and others) for not fulfilling his artistic requirements. Yet the company he would bring to Lincoln Center in 1966 (with a repertory that included nine—*nine!*—new productions, among them Richard Strauss's rarely heard *Die Frau ohne Schatten* and two brand-new American operas) would have challenged in quality any company in the world.

The New York City Opera had been founded in 1943 as a part of Mayor La Guardia's great populist venture, the City Center of Music and Drama, which began life offering plays, ballet, and opera for as little as $1.20 a ticket. Ever since then, the New York City Opera had represented the major alternative to the more expensive grandeur at the Met. In the beginning there was standard grand opera (*Tosca* to start it off, then *Carmen*) done with scrounged or borrowed sets and costumes, some young singers whose eagerness made up for lack of polish, and a few veterans. Encouraged by audience acclaim, the company had soon begun to look beyond the standard repertory; under a series of music directors—Laszlo Halasz, Erich Leinsdorf, Josef Rosenstock, Julius Rudel—it had become a haven for new work, especially new American work. First-rate mountings of scores by Carlisle Floyd, Douglas Moore, Hugo Weisgall, and others had created, really for the first time, the possibility of a native American operatic style.

The enterprising company presented all this to audiences of mostly young opera-goers, informally dressed and wonderfully receptive to new, difficult musical encounters, and always at a very affordable price—in 1962, the best seat in the house went for around $7. Currently, the top price is $35.00, but the least expensive tickets have been held to a very modest $2.40 apiece, and standing room is a mere $2.00.

The City Opera has always prided itself on its dramatic approach to performance; it has prided itself on not having a prompter's box, on not having "stars." In this last regard, its pride has been misplaced—this is the company that has developed its own stars, the likes of Beverly Sills, Placido Domingo, and the late Norman Treigle. It came to

Ballet patron Lincoln Kirstein and the great choreographer George Balanchine (this page) founded the New York City Ballet together in 1948. Over the years, Balanchine created hundreds of original works and rehearsed them with such dancers as (opposite, clockwise from top left) Maria Tallchief, David Richardson, Jacques d'Amboise, Suzanne Farrell, and Peter Martins.

George Balanchine, above, with two members of the corps de ballet, takes a curtain call at the conclusion of the New York City Ballet's spring season, on July 4, 1982.

Lincoln Center on February 22, 1966, with a brand-new opera, a tonsil-breaker: Alberto Ginastera's *Don Rodrigo*, a score written in twelve-tone style. It was just like the City Opera to pull something like that—and to succeed.

In 1948 Morton Baum, chairman of City Center's finance committee and one of that organization's most dedicated movers, asked Lincoln Kirstein, the best friend and patron ballet has ever had, and George Balanchine, one of the most innovative choreographers ever, to form a New York City Ballet Company for City Center. Balanchine, who had worked with Diaghilev in the 1920s, had come to New York in 1933 to found, with Kirstein, the School of American Ballet. He often worked on Broadway (as choreographer for *On Your Toes*, to cite an early success) and joined forces with Kirstein in a number of other short-lived dance ventures. Thanks to the City Center umbrella, there were prospects this time for a longer-lived project, and the present healthy state of the New York City Ballet is the happy result.

The company has always been rigorously trained to

Above left, Jerome Robbins rehearses Patricia McBride in In the Night; *above, Peter Martins rehearses Kyra Nichols and Joseph Duell in* A Schubertiad.

produce nothing short of perfection on its stage; it is surely a measure of the Balanchine temperament that his ballets to music of Stravinsky—most of all the dry-point, neoclassical Stravinsky of *Orpheus*, *Apollo*, and *Agon*—are among his greatest masterpieces. New York has always had a lavish supply of first-rate dance companies—the romantic American Ballet Theatre, the exuberant, youthful Joffrey. Yet the New York City Ballet, with its stunning exactitude, its exaltation of design, its emphasis on clarity of language above all, is the one that sparked the "dance explosion" among American audiences in the 1950s. The company arrived at Lincoln Center on April 23, 1964.

Almost from the beginning, the vision of Lincoln Center included a theatrical ensemble. The magic word *repertory* was often invoked, indicating a compact group of actors who would remain together throughout the season if not beyond, working together to evolve a company style, each actor doing the lead in one play, a smaller role in the next. New York has had its history of repertory, and it has at times been

The Repertory Theater of Lincoln Center spent its first season in this temporary theater just off Washington Square, awaiting completion of the Vivian Beaumont.

glorious, as when Orson Welles had his Mercury Theater, Harold Clurman his Group Theater. Would the Lincoln Center name and the distinction of leadership by Elia Kazan and Robert Whitehead somehow galvanize a new, more lasting repertory ensemble?

Vivian Beaumont Allen promised money to build the repertory theater at Lincoln Center, and it was scheduled to open in 1963. Whitehead and Kazan assembled their company to work toward that time. When building realities forced a two-year postponement, temporary quarters were (literally) dug out of the ground in a vacant lot near the NYU campus in Greenwich Village, creating a subterranean structure designed to the same basic shape and size as the Beaumont-to-be: thrust stage, arena seating. That temporary theater opened on January 13, 1964, with a new play, *After the Fall,* by the distinguished Arthur Miller. The season ended a middling success. The second season opened with a Kazan-directed classic, Thomas Middleton's *The Changeling*, a resounding flop.

Suddenly Lincoln Center was in the news again, but not for the best of reasons. Whitehead and Kazan were out, fired by the Repertory Theater Association. Schuman suggested to the officials of the Repertory Theater a replacement who was already high in management at the Metropolitan Opera, and so Rudolf Bing accused him of "raiding" his staff. Lincoln Center's whole ideal of interaction among its constituents briefly seemed threatened. By the time the ill-fated Repertory Theater moved into Lincoln Center, it was already into its second generation of direction: Jules Irving and Herbert Blau, co-founders of San Francisco's excellent Actors Workshop.

There have been other squabbles along Lincoln Center's way, if not many as masterfully dramatic as in those weeks of hot words and hotter headlines in 1964. But think for a moment: given a roomful of people including two operatic impresarios, a mercurial genius of a choreographer, a spokesman for symphony, and a theater director or two, wouldn't there be something wrong if *nobody* raised his voice?

And there were surely bugs in the Lincoln Center concept; there had to be in so bold a step into the unknown. It made little sense to some commentators to move several of New York's busiest performance organizations into new and untested facilities on a single plot of land with but one subway nearby and few restaurants around. Why, some early

Above, artists and planners discuss the Repertory Theater's future permanent home. Top, Eero Saarinen leans over a drawing; left, Elia Kazan makes a point; center, a model is examined; far right, Kazan muses.

The Vivian Beaumont Theater (below), designed by the Finnish-American architect Eero Saarinen, opened in 1965. In front of it, in the reflecting pool, stands Henry Moore's bronze sculpture Reclining Figure.

Last Tango in Paris, *starring Marlon Brando*

Mean Streets, *starring Robert De Niro*

The Marriage of Maria Braun, *starring Hanna Schygulla (left)*

The Film Society of Lincoln Center, one of the Center's own creations, produces the New York Film Festival which began in 1963. Since then it has introduced a staggering repertory of both foreign and American films to its capacity audiences. Scenes from several are shown here.

Fitzcarraldo, *starring Klaus Kinski*

The American Friend, *starring Dennis Hopper*

naysayers asked, should the Philharmonic, at the height of Leonard Bernstein's popularity, give up Carnegie Hall for a new hall with several hundred fewer seats?

But these criticisms represented a minority view even at the time of ground-breaking, and would remain so. The history of Lincoln Center's early years was one of continual expansion, of never looking back, of blithely ignoring the warnings of the skeptics. The Center's pioneering innovations make a staggering list even today, and some of them have been widely emulated at other centers. During the 1960s the newly created Film Festival became part of Lincoln Center; a resident ensemble of hand-picked virtuosos was created to play chamber music; a network of educational programs was developed to ensure, among other things, the continuance of a Lincoln Center audience in generations to come. And Lincoln Center began its sublime summertime entertainment, the Mostly Mozart concerts, which themselves glowingly justify whatever it took to air-condition the halls and keep them open around the calendar. This beginning of a list of accomplishments at the Center gives at least a partial answer to the questions that, inevitably, began early to resound from culturally concerned citizens the world over.

Perhaps we don't have conclusive answers yet, beyond the dynamics of a typical Lincoln Center evening, something apparent to anyone who passes by. However, there are some significant sidelights. They never did tear down Carnegie Hall. A dedicated citizens' group, led by the violinist Isaac Stern, got the city to purchase and preserve the great old hall, and the impact of Lincoln Center has helped create a new audience so vast that open dates—and empty seats —are now as rare on Fifty-seventh Street as they are six blocks north. What's more, the old and refurbished City Center is busy these nights, too.

3

Live at Lincoln Center

Enough of ancient history for a while; time now for a visit to the Lincoln Center of here and now. We'll take the tour that the tour guides don't offer, one that actually gets us into some of the performances. If you show up for one of the informative Lincoln Center daytime tours you'll get a fascinating backstage look at the costumes being created for the Metropolitan Opera, instruments being tuned at Avery Fisher Hall (as Philharmonic Hall has been known since 1973), a stage being set up at the Vivian Beaumont. But you'll also see nothing but empty seats in those theaters, which means that you'll miss all the vibrations of a live performance. *Our* tour will be different.

Walk in off Columbus Avenue and toward the great center fountain, which was the gift of Charles Revson. The layout of the approach to Lincoln Center is one triumph of Philip Johnson's that nobody has thought to challenge; no arts center anywhere in the country extends a visitor so warm a visual welcome. Up the few steps from the street, across the taxi ramp, and you're enveloped in light from the three great halls that flank the main

Lincoln Center sprang to life on September 23, 1962, when Philharmonic Hall, the first building completed, opened its doors. Here, crowds admire the building from both within and without on that first night.

plaza. Directly ahead is the fountain, one of mankind's most splendid waterworks; radial lines set into the pavement guide our steps toward it—as if guidance were needed. It didn't take long for this roaring, gurgling, manmade cataract (which can be so intricately computer-controlled that people have actually "composed" pieces for it) to become one of the great meeting places on the West Side of Manhattan. On warm nights and cold, it's a place to meet your date, find a date, or simply people-watch. The water-monster may be quiet tonight, but don't be surprised at a sudden gurgle, a roar, a wall of water. (One nearby computer measures the wind velocity and cuts down on the water supply if there is danger of people becoming soaked.)

In warm weather there are other diversions in the plaza as well; it's one of the best-organized outdoor areas in New York, all the better for seeming not organized at all. Youthful musicians, mostly Juilliard students, may start up impromptu outdoor chamber music sessions or even a little jamming—they're encouraged to, and rightly so. In warm-

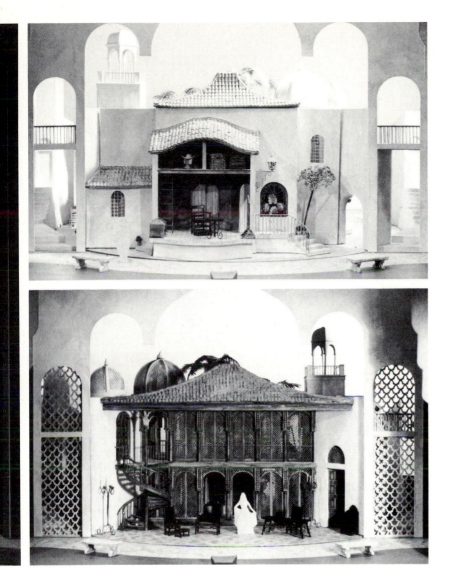

For a recent Met production of The Barber of Seville, *designer Robin Wagner created a single revolving set that rotates on a turntable onstage. At left are models of three of the set's facades.*

weather months there is an ice cream kiosk and even a small alfresco restaurant to complement the agreeable restaurants inside Avery Fisher Hall, the New York State Theater, and the Met. For several weeks each summer there's a joyous festival in the plaza called, simply, Lincoln Center Out-of-Doors. It's a chance to hear first-rate entertainment free of charge, and the fare ranges from a chamber music ensemble from one of the indoor Mostly Mozart programs to an avant-garde dance ensemble from one of the boroughs.

Back at the fountain, facing west, you look at the grand, lit-up façade of the Metropolitan Opera, with its two huge Marc Chagall paintings, which are really seen best from an outdoor vantage point. Other grand music halls stand to your right and left, each with its own distinctive architectural design but both alike in one detail, an outdoor terrace one flight up, so that the people-watchers in the plaza below can themselves be watched. A watcher's paradise, this place.

The Met, you remember, is the grand opera house for international stars; the prices, too, are grand, starting at just $5 for standing room and $13 for seats in the family circle but climbing to $80 for the best seats in the house. Yet among the world's major international houses—Paris, La Scala, Vienna, Covent Garden—the Met's prices are at the low end. And when a typical night might embrace a Verdi masterwork with Placido Domingo and Leontyne Price, or a *La Bohème* with Luciano Pavarotti and Renata Scotto—and a Franco Zeffirelli set that looks as if he's brought over half the city of Paris—the value cannot be measured in mere dollars.

On gala nights—opening night of the season, or the first night of a new production—it's worth the trip to the Met, ticket or no, to watch the patrons thread their way past the photographers and up the spectacular double staircase that is one of the major elements in the building. Inside the auditorium, on any night, the show begins long before the curtain rises, with heated arguments among the standees, operadom's fiercest critics, on the merits of, say, Pavarotti versus Domingo. There's always a great moment just at showtime; the elegant crystal chandeliers, gifts from the government of Austria, pull up toward the scalloped gold ceiling while simultaneously their individual light bulbs are dimmed.

At intermission there is the joy of the promenade. On the concourse level, an exhibit of paintings of past Met stars, usually in their favorite roles. Upstairs on the grand tier level, there is a rather crowded bar; the true aficionado will dash from his seat the moment the curtain falls in order to get his drink on time; latecomers often have to be content with people-watching, which in any case is at its best during a Met intermission.

The lights go down; the house is silent. The conductor threads his way through the orchestra assembled in the pit and bows from his podium to the audience's applause. The stage lights come on and we also see a quick flash of light downstage center, as the prompter in his subterranean box adjusts the mirror that will reveal every corner of the stage and alert him (or her) to where the prompter's helping whisper may be needed. The curtain rises.

Before curtain time, opera-goers at the Met fill (in ascending order) the orchestra-level seats, parterre, grand tier, dress circle, and balcony, above which sits the family circle. The chandeliers rise to the ceiling before the performance.

A scenic artist sketches at his drafting table.

A cannon is prepared for Billy Budd.

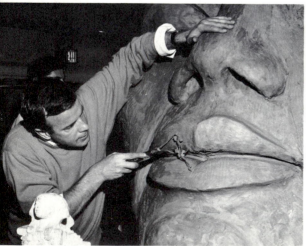

Franco Zeffirelli touches up a Sphinx for Barber's Antony and Cleopatra.

A Chagall drawing for The Magic Flute is rendered full-size by Met artists.

The shops backstage at the Metropolitan Opera House employ more than eighty full-time people, and the photographs on this page give an idea of the variety of work these craftsmen do. Almost everything you see onstage during an opera at the house was made right on the premises.

The grandest Metropolitan sets always get a burst of applause on their own, and most of the Met's sets these days *are* of the grandest. When the house was built, special attention was paid to equipping it for the most lavish kinds of scenic displays—and, just as important, for setting up and removing these displays as quickly as the music itself demanded.

Let's watch from backstage, if we're lucky enough to be invited, to see this process in action, and let's take one of the Met's more difficult productions, Modest Moussorgsky's *Boris Godunov*. The great designer Ming Cho Lee created this production in 1976—a glorious panoply of reds and golds and spectacular stone-enclosed spaces, an ideal visual "orchestration" for the barbaric splendor of the music. But there are many sets; the prologue and first act alone take us from a monastery courtyard to a great cathedral to a monk's cell to a country tavern to Boris's study, and to pause between these scenes for more than a few seconds would destroy the marvelous flow of the music. It is for such a challenge that the new Metropolitan Opera House was designed.

The first scene, in a monastery outside of Moscow, has been set up on the center stage, to be revealed when the curtain first rises. It's amusing to see, backstage, a worker in up-to-date coveralls hammering away on the walls of a medieval cloister, but that's part of the magic of opera, an art which Dr. Samuel Johnson dubbed "exotic and irrational." When the scene ends, the curtain falls momentarily, and the applause of the audience drowns out any noise backstage. Now that whole center stage glides on rails sideways into the wings. At the same time, the second scene, in a great cathedral, glides into place. The Metropolitan Opera's stage actually consists of four stages: the one the audience sees, a space behind it, and another stage on either side, the same size and mounted so that an easy push of a button moves it into place. That way, stage personnel can set up two, even three, scenes at once. These gifted backstage people, perhaps nearly one hundred of them on one set, can transform a cathedral to a tavern before our astonished eyes with almost balletic precision. The deep area backstage can move forward, and the center stage is further mounted so that it can move up and down on elevators.

A night at an opera with many scenes—*Boris Godunov*, or Richard Wagner's *Die Meistersinger*—gives us the chance to experience, if not always to watch, this great ma-

Four men perform one of the heavier jobs of opera-making as they push a piece of a set for Otello *toward its place on stage.*

This cutaway view reveals the enormous backstage area at the Metropolitan Opera House as it might appear during a performance of La Gioconda. Behind and on either side of the main stage, whole sets are made ready to be moved into place. Below the stage level, dressing rooms, practice quarters, and storage space are all in use; on the floors above are numerous construction and maintenance shops.

Ronald A. Mackay

The vast promenade area at the New York State Theater provides a suitably spacious setting for the great pairs of sculpted women by Elie Nadelman that stand at either end.

chinery in action. There is magic in what we see on the stage, but there is further magic in what we cannot see, in the way our imagining can be transported hither and yon with changes so fast as to seem almost instantaneous.

As we leave this great house and head back toward Broadway, Philip Johnson's New York State Theater is on our right; it is the home of the New York City Ballet and the New York City Opera and is also used by touring attractions when those two companies aren't performing.

When we enter its auditorium, we find ourselves in one of the most distinctive spaces in all of Lincoln Center—in all of the world, for that matter. The orchestra seating is in "continental" style, with no center aisle. The five balconies, or "rings" as they are called, are faced with large jewel-like lights; if you're on the stage looking into the house, the effect is a little like facing oncoming headlights on an expressway. Atop the hall is another series of these "headlights," this time resembling nothing so much as some interesting undersea monster.

From wherever you are, check out the seat at the extreme left end of the first ring; that's where Beverly Sills sits on opera nights, her warm, welcoming smile brighter than any of those headlights.

The City Opera under Beverly Sills, who assumed the general directorship in 1979, has slowed somewhat its former pace in presenting brand-new American operas, but it continues to explore the more serious Broadway fare, with a popular revival of Leonard Bernstein's *Candide* to its recent credit and Stephen Sondheim's *Sweeney Todd* in 1984. Guided by Sills, the company has sought adventure in other kinds of unfamiliar repertory, including great European scores of the recent past suffering undeserved neglect. One of its spectacular recent triumphs along this line was a production of Leoš Janáček's woodland fantasy *The Cunning Little Vixen*, a fabulously beautiful score composed for both human and animal characters and produced at the State Theater with sets and costumes by the wonderful children's illustrator Maurice Sendak. If it's on the bill, don't miss it. Even if it isn't, there's always the continuing delight at the City Opera of the chance to discover some rising young singer whose name is just becoming known. Current bright lights include bass Samuel Ramey, tenor Jerry Hadley, and sopranos Gianna Rolandi and Carol Vaness.

While you're at the State Theater, don't miss the huge promenade (up one flight from plaza level). Bigger than some

whole theaters, it's easily the most attractive lobby in the entire Lincoln Center complex.

Since prices are lower at the State Theater than at the Met, the crowd tends to be more informal and somewhat younger. That holds on ballet nights, too. The subtle classicism of Balanchine's pristine choreography remains in the repertory; a night with one of his great Stravinsky ballets is one of life's most refined aesthetic experiences. Now there is new leadership—the great *danseur noble* Peter Martins and the sublimely versatile choreographer Jerome Robbins, who has contributed some superb works to the New York City Ballet repertory. Changes in the temperament of the City Ballet's work, but not in its level of excellence, are sure to come.

Across from the State Theater, at the north side of the plaza, is the Lincoln Center building that was the first to open, Avery Fisher Hall, home of the Philharmonic (the oldest symphony orchestra in the United States), and home-away-from-home to a host of visiting orchestras, recital artists, even chamber groups.

Inside the plaza-level lobby, pandemonium is the usual order of things. Perhaps this is a night when Zubin Mehta, the Philharmonic's current music director, has programmed one of his specialties—Mahler or Strauss—and no tickets are to be had. A long line at one box-office window waits for canceled tickets that will be distributed through an orderly process as they become available. Elsewhere in the lobby, other ticketless hopefuls stare at arriving concert-goers with

Alice Tully Hall (opposite) provides an ideal place for hearing chamber music, small orchestras, and soloists.

Top soloists who like to play together form the Chamber Music Society (left).

Since being rebuilt in 1976, the inside of Avery Fisher Hall is a boxlike space (above), shaped like many traditional concert halls; originally (inset) the room had curved walls, and acoustical "clouds" hung from the ceiling.

unconcealed envy. Behind the scenes, underneath the stage, more than one hundred musicians warm up and tune their instruments, and as 8:00 P.M. approaches, the maestro prepares for his slow elevator ride to the stage entrance.

In its series of changes from acoustical ugly duckling to first-rate sounding board—a story for a later chapter—Avery Fisher Hall has gone through startling changes of appearance. It began life as a long, relatively narrow room of blue and gold; in an intermediate stage it was sheathed in natural wood tones with the upholstery in maroon; now

it is a gleaming palace of off-white and old gold, with even its basic shape altered. One element remains constant, however; it has always been a comfortable house for players and for listeners. The spacious orchestra-level lobby seems to accommodate everybody without crowding, and over this space hangs one of the most remarkable of Lincoln Center's sculptural treasures, a pair of abstractions, constructed of metal plates, by Richard Lippold, representing the god Apollo imparting to the sweet singer Orpheus the gift of music.

It's not only Apollo or the Philharmonic, however, who hands out gifts of music at Avery Fisher Hall. In summer, the Mostly Mozart concerts take over, forty-two of them each year, one of Lincoln Center's most successful programming innovations and one that has been widely copied by orchestras across the country. The programs concentrate on eighteenth- and early-nineteenth-century music, the kind that sounds best with an orchestra of thirty or so, and they are full of exploration: an unknown early Haydn symphony, one of Mozart's youthful operas in concert performance, a Handel or Haydn oratorio with a small chorus joining in, a combined song and chamber music recital—even the American première of a long-lost Mozart symphony. The prices are low, the audience is knowledgeable; night after night for seven or eight weeks each summer, Mostly Mozart is one of New York's hottest ticket items.

Head north from Avery Fisher Hall, cross Sixty-fifth Street, and you come to the building shared by Alice Tully Hall—the chamber music hall that was once going to be tucked into Avery Fisher Hall—and the Juilliard School. Juilliard is, in the words of its late president Peter Mennin, "Lincoln Center's professional training arm." Its name was the Juilliard School of Music until 1969, when it moved downtown from its old home on Claremont Avenue and expanded to become a cornerstone in New York's theater, music, and dance life. Now it is simply the Juilliard School. Its building —including Alice Tully Hall—was designed by architect Pietro Belluschi.

The noble Alice Tully, a one-time singer and now a full-time great lady, a music-lover with money to spend and wisdom about how to spend it, funded the building of the lovely, warm-hearted auditorium that bears her name. Later, she spent some more money to give the hall a proper pipe organ, a splendid, relatively small instrument in keeping with the intimacy of the room.

Alice Tully Hall is the place for the intimate recital:

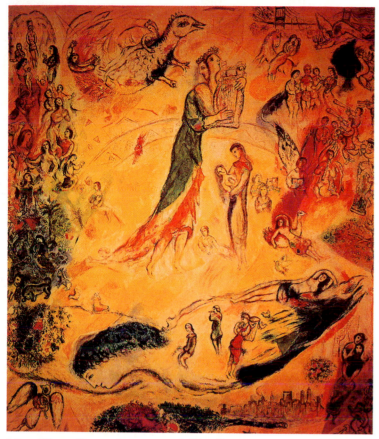

Marc Chagall's two huge murals The Sources of Music *(above) and* The Triumph of Music *(below) cover the two front walls of the Met's lobby and are grandly visible from both inside and outside the house.*

Richard Lippold's glittering sculpture Orpheus and Apollo *floa*

ove the lobby of Avery Fisher Hall.

a program of Schubert songs; a Beethoven Quartet cycle by the Guarneri or Juilliard quartet; a sold-out series by Alice Tully's resident ensemble, the Chamber Music Society of Lincoln Center. The success of the Society, organized in 1969 by the pianist Charles Wadsworth, has been phenomenal. The Society has captured a crowd whose ears have become saturated with the big symphonic sound and who want instead the intellectual stimulation of music built to a more personal scale.

There have always been chamber concerts in New York, and always many that sold out. One thinks back to the 1930s and '40s—the typical audience at chamber music concerts then was elderly, opinionated, and usually foreign-born; a young native in attendance was looked upon as a rash intruder. Applause after a particularly notable rendition might rise to the level of a soft rustle. Now look at the crowd at Alice Tully Hall for tonight's Chamber Music Society concert: informally dressed, many listeners college-age or even younger joining the older music lovers. Overheard conversations reveal a real chamber music connoisseurship, and a great performance will draw cheers. It helps that Wadsworth himself, a pianist of great sensitivity and a person of wit with an infectious Georgia drawl, frequently comes onstage before the concert to welcome the crowd.

The Chamber Music Society just happened to strike the right programming chord at the right time, and its volume has been increasing ever since. The continuing audience loyalty the Society enjoys after fifteen years of virtually sold-out concerts suggests that someone in the organization is doing something right.

That's not quite all of Lincoln Center; we've missed two important corners. At the southwest corner stands a curious structure that turns out to be the bandshell at Damrosch Park (named after a whole family of musicians important to the history of New York music). Here concerts by military and brass bands—or, at times, semiprofessional opera companies—take place on summer nights. Picnic lunches (or dinners, or perhaps even breakfasts) seem to taste especially good on the benches among the flowering azaleas here—this corner offers an unstructured refuge to set off

The pool, with Henry Moore's Reclining Figure, *presents a peaceful scene during a February snowfall.*

The Guggenheim Bandshell, in Damrosch Park, is the setting for Lincoln Center Out-of-Doors concerts, as seen here, and other free events.

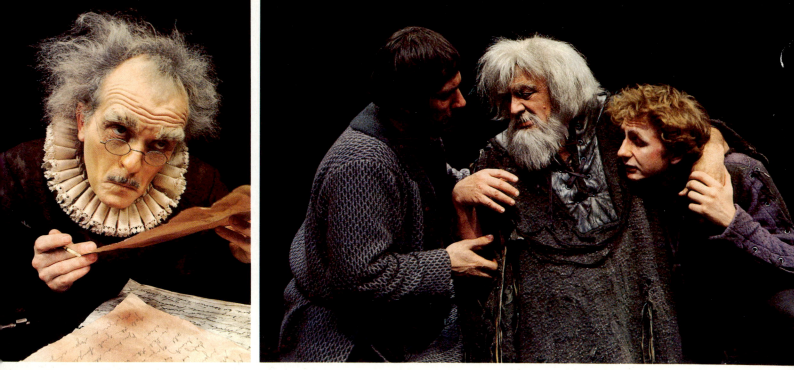

The Miser

King Lear

The Tragedy of Carmen

The Philadelphia Story

the rest of Lincoln Center's highly structured life.

And there is life at the northwest corner, too, structured and otherwise. Skirting the reflecting pool, with its Henry Moore *Reclining Figure*, we then pass by a spiderlike Alexander Calder stabile, *Le Guichet* ("Box office"), and we enter the quiet sanctuary of the New York Public Library at Lincoln Center, Library & Museum of the Performing Arts. On open shelves on the first floor there's a splendid selection of books on the performing arts, a huge circulating record collection, and a fine store of printed music. The Orchestra Collection provides scores and parts to amateur and semi-professional orchestras in the metropolitan area. One flight up is an exhibition space where a collection of great operatic set models or costumes might be on show, or a priceless collection of Stravinsky letters and manuscripts. Another second-floor treasure is the children's library, with a charming walled-in space, the Heckscher Oval, where story-reading hours are often held.

On the top floor is one of the world's foremost research libraries—again devoted to material in music, theater, and dance, and including the wondrous Rodgers and Hammerstein Archives of Recorded Sound. When you want to know how Arturo Toscanini conducted at the Salzburg Festival in pre-Hitler years, you check it out on a tape in the Rodgers and Hammerstein collection. The tape is there because someone in 1936 thought to record the performance off his shortwave radio.

The library building is contiguous with the embattled Vivian Beaumont Theater, which also contains a small performance space, the Mitzi E. Newhouse Theater, downstairs. Although the Beaumont has been closed more often than open in the past few years, it reopened excitingly in the fall of 1983 with Peter Brook's *The Tragedy of Carmen*. For this production, the stage of the theater was raised and covered with a layer of sand. Anyone seated in the front rows really felt himself at the edge of a desert, with the drama of Carmen and her hapless suitor played out almost at his feet. It was a controversial, immensely theatrical production, and gave the Beaumont theater the excitement it was built to house.

The Vivian Beaumont Theater has played host to many outstanding dramatic performances, most recently Peter Brook's The Tragedy of Carmen, *based on the Bizet opera* Carmen. *Scenes from several Beaumont Theater successes are shown here.*

The Threepenny Opera

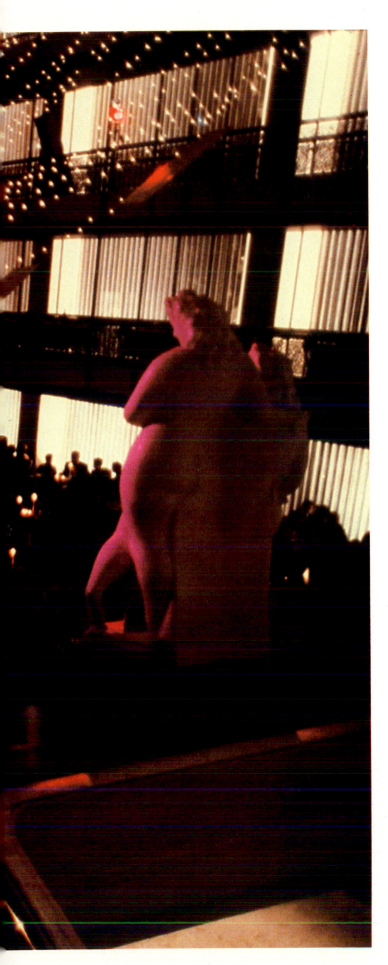

4
Men, Women, and Money

It's a gala night at Lincoln Center, with an operatic première, say, or an illustrious guest soloist at the Philharmonic. Tickets have been sold out for weeks; even the standing room is jam-packed. To an outsider looking in at such a scene, the performing arts appear to be making money hand over fist. The outsider would, however, be wrong.

The arts have never paid their way. From the Middle Ages right up to our own time, the bills have always been footed by some kind of aristocracy. The glorious cultural panoply that bedazzles the visitor to Florence, for example, is a lasting monument to the benevolence of nobles such as the Medici family who vied for immortality during the Renaissance. The *Brandenburg* Concertos of Johann Sebastian Bach, most of the symphonies and quartets of Franz Joseph Haydn, the magnificent drama of Richard Wagner's *Ring of the Nibelung*—all these masterworks exist only because somebody with money and taste happened along to offer these composers a fair compensation for their work.

That work has always been expensive, too. Drawings and paintings that

On May 21, 1979, the twentieth anniversary of the groundbreaking for Lincoln Center was celebrated with twin parties —this grand affair in the promenade at the New York State Theater and a similar one across the way at Avery Fisher.

survive from opera's early days—in Mantua, Florence, Venice, later throughout Europe—show productions of consummate splendor, lavish scenic effects and costumes. As opera became popular, so did its leading singers, so that they could command fabulous fees wherever they were engaged. None of this has changed. A top singer in an American house can now command as much as $15,000 for an evening's warbling.

And consider that on Broadway you'll see a dazzling show in which one star and one co-star perform on one set all evening; a typical grand-opera production is infinitely more complicated. Usually, everything you view on stage at the Met was especially designed and—except for the singers' shoes—made by the company. The cost of a single night at the opera can run to six figures, more than the box-office take. If this seems excessive, go backstage and see what it takes to create the illusions, the magic, that we see from out front. Watch how an opera at the Met, or even at the State Theater, where backstage facilities are more modest, seems to float along effortlessly from one magnificent tableau to the next. It only takes a few moments of breathtaking spectacle to prove that the cost isn't excessive.

On the other hand, a composer who gets a commission for a new symphony can spend most of his fee having orchestral parts copied, because orchestras cannot afford their own staffs of music copyists. So while songbirds and other top virtuosos may come out ahead, opera companies, symphony managements, and composers couldn't make it through a season if it weren't for some form of outside subsidy.

You might argue that at $80 a ticket the Metropolitan Opera should be able to afford anything, and perhaps if every ticket in the house went for $80, the opera really could pay its way. But only 3 per cent of the seats command those top prices; most go for far less. Lincoln Center and its constituents, like all performing-arts organizations, are committed to keeping prices down, to keep the arts accessible. So a sellout at the box office falls far short of paying for an event at Lincoln Center or anywhere else. In the 1982/83 season the projection for combined ticket sales at Lincoln Center came to nearly $59 million, against a projected $85 million for nothing more than merely getting all those performances on and off the stage—and that doesn't count all the unseen, unglamorous expenses: building maintenance and personnel, administrative costs, and the like.

Somebody has to pay. In Europe, national governments have long since assumed the role that the nobility used to

PICTURING PERFORMANCE

Over the years, Lincoln Center for the Performing Arts, Inc., has commissioned an impressive array of posters from some of the nation's most respected artists. Six are shown on the following pages; the creators of others include Frank Stella, Robert Indiana, and Larry Rivers.

LINCOLN CENTER
FOR THE PERFORMING ARTS

PHILHARMONIC HALL
OPENING SEPTEMBER 23, 1962

By Ben Shahn

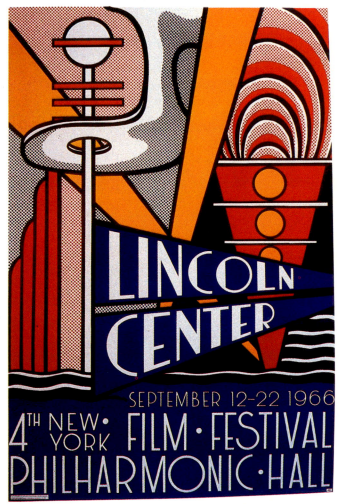

By Roy Lichtenstein

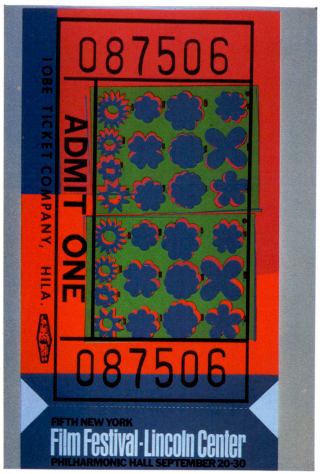

By Andy Warhol

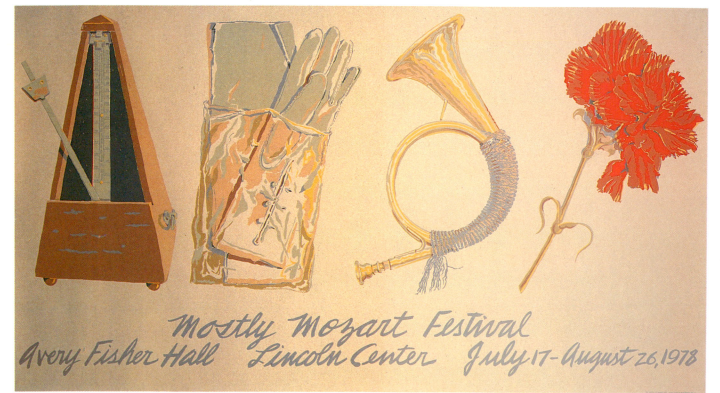

By Don Nice

70

MOSTLY MOZART FESTIVAL

AVERY FISHER HALL, LINCOLN CENTER

JULY 14—AUGUST 23, 1980

By Dan Christensen

The latest poster in the series, for the 1984 Mostly Mozart Festival, is by the artist Fernando Botero.

play. In Paris, you couldn't make a private donation to the Opéra even if you wanted to; it's illegal. West Germany obliges every citizen to buy an owner's license for radios and TV sets as we do for automobiles, and that tax is directly earmarked for supporting the nation's orchestras and opera houses.

The United States has made some strides toward governmental participation in the arts both federally and on the state level, but there exists nothing as yet like the support enjoyed in European countries, and the available funds are extremely changeable from year to year, executive to executive. Of the total expenses of Lincoln Center and its constituents in the 1982/83 fiscal year, some $150 million, government grants covered only about 5 per cent. Yet that makes a certain sense. The American aristocracy that once supported culture were members of an industrial, commercial, corporate, and private aristocracy, and their heritage is the web of corporate and private funding out of which great cultural monuments like Lincoln Center can and do come.

Private support of the arts in America assumes a variety of sizes and shapes. Opera-goers are accustomed to finding the name of a principal donor on the program page whenever the Metropolitan or New York City Opera companies offer a new production. At the Met, new productions of *La Bohème*, *Francesca da Rimini*, and the planned-for-1985 *Tosca* all bear the name of Sybil Harrington, widow of Texas oil investor Donald D. Harrington and a long-time, avid, exceptionally modest patron of grand opera. The company's astounding, controversial production of Wagner's *Ring of the Nibelung* bore the patronage of Eastern Airlines. Other productions at both Lincoln Center houses have been underwritten by out-of-town sources such as Cincinnati's Corbett Foundation and the Gramma Fisher Foundation of Marshalltown, Iowa, both of them run by fine gentlemen afflicted with a wondrous, incurable passion for opera.

To build a vast cultural complex, however, and to equip its buildings for putting on a panorama of cultural entertainments—this requires a lot more than the cost of an individual opera production, and it takes the vision of far more distant horizons. Most of the buildings had to be financed by the private sector. Where was that kind of money to come from in the 1950s?

As the answer began to emerge, one familiar name towered, as usual, above the rest: the Rockefeller family. It was Nelson Rockefeller, as visible, audible, and exuberant a

The New York City Ballet's elaborate Christmas-season performances of The Nutcracker *have become one of Lincoln Center's most beloved traditions, especially for children and their families. Scenes from recent performances of the Tchaikovsky masterpiece are shown on these two pages.*

patron as the arts have ever enjoyed, who as governor of New York State established the pioneering venture of cultural subsidy on the state level; his New York State Council for the Arts, set up in 1960, has now been imitated in every state of the Union. Before Nelson there had been John D., Jr., whose land, whose millions, whose dreams, had gone into the erection of the grand midtown project Rockefeller Center, which in some ways served as a trial run for Lincoln Center. And his son John D. 3rd served as the spark to get Lincoln Center both on and off the ground. With fine paternal benevolence, John D., Jr., bestowed ten of his millions on the project in its days aborning; as for John D. 3rd, his gifts during his leadership at Lincoln Center amounted, at conservative estimate, to something like $12 million. Clearly the Rockefellers were still at the Center, where they truly belonged.

The very visibility of the Lincoln Center project from its beginning galvanized the money of New York as it did the imaginings of hopeful hordes of symphony- and opera-goers of whatever economic level. Here, after all, was the opportunity to spend money in the full glare of publicity, and to ensure that it went for the greatest public good.

It was the wonderful Eleanor Belmont, for example, who established and funded the early years of the Metropolitan Opera Guild, which gave the Met the first organized fund-raising arm in its history. Mrs. Belmont died in 1979 at the age of 101; she lived to see and enjoy the room on the Met's grand tier dedicated in her name—a private room of great charm and beauty, like its namesake.

And the efforts of other great women helped immeasurably as Lincoln Center's first organizers struggled through the years of planning and building. Vivian Beaumont Allen was approached during the first wave of fund-raising for possible help in funding a home for the new Repertory Theater. Mrs. Allen was willing, but she wasn't what you'd call a soft touch. She is known to have hated the locating of "her" theater at the back of the building site, far removed from the confluence of the three great music halls, and was won over only by the excellence of the design by architect Eero Saarinen. Mrs. Allen's gift of $3 million toward the theater that bears her name was one of Lincoln Center's most glowing early votes of confidence.

As early as 1957 Alice Tully had expressed her desire to contribute anonymously to the building of a chamber music

More than 200 people fill the stage for the Christmas Eve party in Act II of the Metropolitan Opera's lavish La Bohème, *designed and produced by Franco Zeffirelli.*

In 1981 the English artist David Hockney provided the designs for "Parade: An Evening of French Music Theater," at the Met. Above is his sketch for Les Mamelles de Tirésias, *by Francis Poulenc; opposite, a study for the set of* L'Enfant et les sortilèges, *by Maurice Ravel.*

hall, which was at that time penciled in for inclusion within Philharmonic Hall. By 1965, when a more ambitious small hall had been incorporated instead into the Juilliard building to the north of the plaza, Miss Tully let it be known that she would increase her contribution; she also acquiesced in the use of her name for the hall.

And there were more, many more, great patrons: a $10 million bequest in 1971 from yet another bearer of that great name, the cultural philanthropist Martha Baird Rockefeller; a $4.4 million grant that same year from the Edna McConnell Clark Foundation, earmarked for educational programs.

But Lincoln Center's benefactors weren't all on the distaff side. Another $10 million beneficence came in 1973 from Avery Fisher, to endow fellowship awards for significant young musicians and also to make possible the final redesign and acoustic repair of the hall that now bears his name. Mr. Fisher, one of the first manufacturers to make the world aware of the potential of quality high-fidelity components,

likes to identify his donation as "the repayment of a personal debt." "I owed something to music," he says. As simple as that.

The years of Lincoln Center, in fact, have been the years when all Americans, as individuals or as corporate leaders, finally began to face up to the responsibility of paying the bills for culture that the arts themselves could never pay. The honor roll of Lincoln Center is vast; you see it inscribed on stone tablets in the lobbies of the great halls, on metal plaques on the backs of seats...and, more important still, in the rich glow around every sound from every stage. The superb sound that exists today in the New York State Theater, for example, stems from the magnanimity of the Fan Fox and Leslie R. Samuels Foundation, which in 1982 underwrote that hall's badly needed acoustic overhaul. When the sound of Lincoln Center comes into our homes via live telecasts from its halls, we must thank the underwriting of these series by Exxon (which maintains the "Live From Lincoln Center" telecasts) and Texaco (which has been the Metropolitan Opera's sponsor, on radio and TV, for nearly half a century). No fewer than thirty-four of America's leading corporate executives were brought together to spearhead the latest annual Lincoln Center Consolidated Corporate Fund Drive, under the chairmanship of the Chase Manhattan Bank's persuasive chairman, Willard C. Butcher. The Consolidated Corporate Fund Drive was founded in 1969, when it raised $870,000. In fiscal 1983 it raised $3.8 million; altogether, corporations gave $8.8 million to Lincoln Center, Inc., and its constituents that year.

Lincoln Center's biggest source of contribution support is individuals, and they gave a total of $15.4 million in 1983. One recent program designed both to spur individuals to make larger donations and to thank them for their help is the Chairman's Council, created two years ago. The Chairman's Council invites all donors of $2,000 a year or more to be members, and rewards them with invitations to special gala occasions at the Center at which cocktails and dinner are served and major Lincoln Center artists are introduced.

Wherever you look—at the great buildings of Lincoln Center inside and out, even on the pages of the program books for individual events—you see the shape of the place as a glowing monument to an enlightened citizenry and its dedication to the arts. For example, the page of the Avery Fisher Hall program listing the performers' roster of the New York Philharmonic shows that many of the first-desk players' salaries are endowed by individual donors. Concertmaster Glenn Dicterow sits in the Charles E. Culpeper Chair; first cellist Lorne Munroe performs from a chair (in other words, a position) endowed by the same Fox-Samuels Foundation that saw to the State Theater renovation; the chair of principal flutist Jeanne Baxtresser is secured by an endowment from the late Lila Acheson Wallace, co-founder of *The Reader's Digest* and a long-time lover of the performing arts. Many guest artists' appearances at the Philharmonic are made possible through the Hedwig van Ameringen Guest Artists Endowment Fund. And across the street, the Chamber Music Society has six endowed chairs, each representing a contribution of $250,000 or more to provide permanent support for one of the instrumental positions required by works in the chamber music repertoire.

And so it goes, throughout the financial structure—shaky still, of course, but remarkably well tended to—of Lincoln Center's operation. Great and deservedly famous peo-

Each spring, the Film Society of Lincoln Center holds a special gala evening at Avery Fisher Hall to honor a distinguished film artist. The event includes reminiscences by colleagues and a showing of excerpts from the artist's films. These photos were taken on the evenings that honored Charles Chaplin and Alfred Hitchcock (right).

ple are involved, but so are others whose love affair with the arts has gone on outside the spotlights of fame.

Many donations demonstrate the way the culturally aware people of a great city have taken the prospects of Lincoln Center into their own lives. One day in 1962 the management was informed of a $1 million bequest from a certain Mrs. Hazel Hopkins Ford. Who was she? Nobody in cultural circles seemed to know; she had been a recluse, tended to in a small East Side apartment by a nurse. But she loved music and thrilled to the promise of Lincoln Center. For years she had asked her nurse nearly every day to drive her past the construction site; now, silently, she offered her tribute. Out of such gestures, some made in the arena of publicity, some silently, almost surreptitiously, has the Lincoln Center dream been guided toward reality and allowed to continue to grow.

Charles Chaplin

François Truffaut, Grace Kelly, and Alfred Hitchcock with Martin E. Segal

5

Fulfillment

The buildings at Lincoln Center opened their doors one by one over a period of seven years almost to the day, from Philharmonic Hall on September 23, 1962, to the Juilliard School on October 26, 1969. Anyone who was living in New York remembers those seven years as a series of mounting waves of excitement, each cresting on a note of triumph as the components of Lincoln Center surmounted all obstacles to welcome their first audiences.

Those first days in the new houses were heady ones—the New York Philharmonic's musicians could talk of little but the joy of air-conditioned backstage changing rooms; new production after new production at the Met came off as a magician's feat because of the house's stage equipment; audiences at Alice Tully Hall discovered they could hear chamber music without the roar of street traffic; hopeful young musicians at Juilliard, in their centrally located building, found they could glean knowledge and inspiration from their newly gained proximity to America's musical center. Anyone who experienced that period was quick to realize how badly Lincoln Center had been needed and how triumphantly it was answering those needs.

Zubin Mehta conducts the Philharmonic and eleven-year-old pianist Joel Fan in a Young People's Concert in 1980.

Nearly a quarter of a million people look on as fireworks light up the sky over New York's Central Park to accompany a Philharmonic performance of Tchaikovsky's 1812 Over-ture *during a free summer concert in July 1982.*

83

Leonard Bernstein (right) consults with composer Aaron Copland during "Tuning Week" prior to the opening of Philharmonic Hall, in late September, 1962.

As each building opened, the novel concept of Lincoln Center as a creative force in and of itself working side by side with its constituents became ever more real. The allure of Philharmonic Hall was, primarily, that it afforded the New York Philharmonic a home at last. Yet some of Lincoln Center's own creations— the Film Society and Mostly Mozart, to name two—also made their home at this first new hall. Thus each building in turn stood not merely *in* Lincoln Center, but also *of* Lincoln Center. The realization of this spelled a new era for the performing arts in America.

Five major buildings make up the Lincoln Center complex—seven building units, actually, since Juilliard and Alice Tully Hall are housed under the same roof, and the New York Public Library and the Vivian Beaumont Theater are also in a single structure. Each has had its own record of accomplishment since its opening; each, therefore, tells its own separate story.

Philharmonic (now Avery Fisher) Hall—On September 23, 1962, Lincoln Center's gala first audience had to pick its way through a few last piles of construction debris, but none of this mattered as Leonard Bernstein led his Philharmonic, a chorus, and a capacity audience in a thunderous, exultant national anthem to start the program. It was a night for music. The fare was chosen to capture the exhilaration of the event but also to give the hall's acoustics a definitive shakedown: movements from Mahler's Eighth Symphony and Beethoven's *Missa solemnis*, a new work by the beloved Aaron Copland, and Vaughan Williams's haunting invocation to the lyric art, his *Serenade to Music*. Some critics found the program something of a patchwork, but its celebratory content was never in doubt. The matter of the acoustics, however, raised considerable doubts. The sound, many listeners and musicians felt, was harsh and unnatural; players on the stage complained that they couldn't hear themselves or one another. It would not be until after several minor rebuildings and then, in 1976, the total revamping subsidized by benefactor Avery Fisher—and engineered by acoustician Cyril Harris— that the hall reached its hoped-for sonic splendor.

Even before its acoustic problems were solved, the hall became a great stimulus for the Philharmonic to update its whole musical philosophy, to try out a few new ideas. Some of these "experiments" didn't last, except in fond memories: André Kostelanetz leading the Philharmonic in a springtime series of lighter-weight "Promenade" concerts, with orchestra seats replaced by tables for light refreshments; Pierre

Boulez, in his time as the Philharmonic's music director, putting on concerts of hard-edged new music with the downstairs audience seated on foam-rubber "rugs," again to impart an air of informality and bring orchestra and audience somewhat closer together.

The "Proms" and the "Rugs" are gone, but they achieved their purpose in luring more and more people to live symphonic concerts. Today's Philharmonic audiences number many of those people, and seldom in its history has its box-office appeal been stronger. Zubin Mehta, its current director, first gained international attention in 1958, when at twenty-two he took first prize in the Liverpool International Conductor's Competition. By 1960 he was substituting for great maestros all over the world, and by 1962 he was music director of two major orchestras, the Montreal Symphony and the Los Angeles Philharmonic. He has since become music director of the Israel Philharmonic and has appeared with the Met numerous times. He became music director of the New York Philharmonic in 1978. He shares with his predecessors Bernstein and Boulez a passion for creating thrilling musical drama out of the abstractions of a classic symphony, a romantic concerto, or a piece from the avant-garde. When Mehta is involved with one of his specialties, an emotion-charged Mahler symphony or one of the galloping tone-poems of Richard Strauss, you can almost imagine that Avery Fisher Hall itself has taken wing.

Currently, the Philharmonic has redoubled its efforts to keep itself and its audiences abreast of new musical ideas. Thanks to a grant program administered by Exxon and the Rockefeller Foundation, a resident composer is now part of the Philharmonic staff, creating new music for the orchestra and, even more important, arranging an annual series of new-music concerts. In the summer of 1983, resident composer Jacob Druckman served as artistic director of the first of these Horizons festivals, a long string of events including a thrilling sweep through brand-new music, most but not all of it American. The concerts were surprisingly well-attended: the old saw "The easiest way to clear an auditorium is to play something new" has lost some of its teeth. There were seminars at which audiences could glare at composers and ask pointed questions about musical content and intent; the effect of it all was to break down remarkably the traditional wall between the creative artist and the audience of his own time. Clearly the Horizons concerts mark a major new venture for the Philharmonic.

In June 1982 the Avery Fisher Hall stage was specially expanded for a joint performance by the New York and Israel Philharmonics of Berlioz's Symphonie fantastique. *Zubin Mehta conducted 220 musicians.*

There has been a great sense of growth in the Philharmonic in its years at Lincoln Center—a broadened scope in programming, broadened audience appeal, and, consequently, a great upsurge in activities. The orchestra has taken its music far afield—in the summer of 1984 it toured Asia for five and a half weeks, visiting such cities as Delhi, Bombay, Calcutta, Tokyo, and Singapore. The year before, the orchestra traveled to ten cities across the United States; in 1982, to six nations of South America. Closer to home, the Philharmonic has completed sixty consecutive seasons of Young People's Concerts, continues to give free concerts in the parks and at Harlem's Abyssinian Baptist Church, gives a joint concert each year with the All-City High School Orchestra, and maintains its own charitable trust, the Music Assistance Fund, for minority orchestral musicians. In its twenty years at Lincoln Center the Philharmonic has given over 3,800 concerts, achieving its 10,000th during the 1982/83 season. That's nearly 4,000 concerts in twenty years, as against just over 6,000 in the previous 120 years!

But never mind figures. Come to Avery Fisher Hall on a day when thousands of school children have been bussed in to hear Zubin Mehta conduct programs for tomorrow's subscribers. Walk over to Central Park on a night when the orchestra gives one of its free concerts there. More than 7.2 million people have attended these concerts over the years. Or watch the Philharmonic at home. The Philharmonic, with André Previn on the podium and Van Cliburn as soloist, gave the first "Live From Lincoln Center" telecast in 1976; in the winter of 1983/84, with Zubin Mehta conducting and James Galway as soloist, it performed the fiftieth.

New York State Theater—On April 23, 1964, Lincoln Center opened its second major hall, built as New York State's contribution to the World's Fair. Philip Johnson's design was generally admired, especially the handsome second-floor-level promenade flanked by two massive Elie Nadelman sculptures donated by Mr. Johnson. As at Philharmonic Hall, the opening-night program was a showcase to demonstrate the great variety that that vast stage could accommodate. George Balanchine's New York City Ballet participated in the inaugural festivities with two of Balanchine's own ballets, *Allegro Brillante* and *Stars and Stripes*. The newly formed Music Theater also contributed, with a scene from Richard Rodgers and Oscar Hammerstein's *Carousel*.

The acoustic problems on the other side of the Lincoln Center plaza had made New York's audience edgily perceptive on the subject, and before long it turned out that here, too, there were problems. They were never as serious as Philharmonic Hall's, but they came into greater prominence when the City Opera followed the New York City Ballet into the theater with an opening-night world première of Alberto Ginastera's *Don Rodrigo*, which starred a young City Opera discovery named Placido Domingo. Eventually a major acoustic overhaul was accomplished, directed by the man who had restored Avery Fisher Hall to acoustic credibility, Cyril Harris, and generously underwritten by the Fan Fox and Leslie R. Samuels Foundation.

The Rodgers Music Theater project survived until 1970 and was marked by some spectacular revivals of distinguished Broadway fare, including *West Side Story* and Rodgers and Hammerstein's own *The King and I*. The demise of the Music

Mehta (above) became music director of the Philharmonic in 1978; his contract now extends into 1990, which will make him the longest tenured music director in the Philharmonic's history.

Eileen Schauler plays the queen in the New York City Opera production of Josef Tal's Ashmedai.

Beverly Sills performs in the title role of Menotti's La Loca, *at the City Opera in 1979.*

Theater was a decided loss but was made bearable by the success of the City Opera, with its own broad definition of operatic fare. Under Julius Rudel's leadership the company had always been noted for its ventures into contemporary opera and into masterpieces of the musical theater. George Gershwin's *Porgy and Bess* had been a City Opera standard for years, as had Kurt Weill's *Street Scene.* When Beverly Sills acceded to Rudel's position, in 1979, she announced a continuation of the Broadway connection, with a lively revival of Bernstein's *Candide* in 1982 and a production of Stephen Sondheim's *Sweeney Todd* slated for 1984.

By the early 1960s the City Opera had become the flagship for a vast program of commissions for new operas, sponsored by the Ford Foundation. Would the company, in leaving the dowdy, inexpensive City Center, lose some of that sense of adventure? By choosing *Don Rodrigo* as its first work at Lincoln Center the City Opera answered those fears. Since the Ford Foundation project wound down there haven't been as many brand-new works at the City Opera as there once were. (Philip Glass's *Akhnaten* is, however, in preparation for the fall of 1984.) But, with such rollicking fare as *Candide* and such superb rediscoveries as Handel's *Alcina,* Mozart's *La Clemenza di Tito,* and several powerful scores by the Czech master Leoš Janáček, it would be hard to fault the company as the originator of some of the most adventurous operatic productions in our time.

Ever since Beverly Sills took over, she has been working to make the City Opera even more accessible to its audience. The prices of all subscriptions were reduced by 20 per cent in 1982, and all seats for opening night of 1984 went for $2.40, the same price as on opening night in 1944, the company's first season forty years before. In 1983, the City Opera began to experiment with the projection of subtitles above the proscenium, providing instant translations of foreign dialogue. The innovation proved an immediate success, and subtitles are now being used with every non-English-language opera the company performs. The City Opera is even arranging to make them available to other companies. Yet another recent development was the founding of the City Opera National Company. It has now completed four national tours, and in 1984 it visited seventeen states.

If the City Opera reigns supreme in just one area, it is the discovery of bright, new operatic singers. Beverly Sills likes to call the City Opera a "feeder" for the large international houses. She, Norman Treigle, Placido Domingo,

Sherrill Milnes, and a vast array of other star-quality talents were discovered at the City Opera, and the sense of discovery continues. The City Opera has always been accessible to young singers, and they continue to come in through the back door as unknowns and go out the front door as stars.

In many ways the New York City Ballet shares the philosophy of its companion company, but there are major differences as well. Founded by the legendary George Balanchine, funded at first almost single-handedly by Lincoln Kirstein, the New York City Ballet was always intended to serve, above all, as a showcase for Balanchine's sublime, distinctive, creative art. The company has always used guest choreographers, including a few—John Clifford, head of the Los Angeles Ballet, for one—who as dancers grew up through the company's ranks. The marvelous Jerome Robbins' history in dance goes back at least to his collaboration with Leonard Bernstein in the 1944 *Fancy Free*, which gave American-created ballet its first toehold in the international market; he has created some of his most appealing ballets for Balanchine's company, including the ineffably lovely *Dances at a Gathering* and *The Goldberg Variations*. But the New York City Ballet was Balanchine's sketchpad, and with it he created a store of dance masterworks unchallenged by any living choreographer, including a whole repertory of ballets to the music of Stravinsky, which came together in two astonishing Stravinsky Festivals, the first in the year after the composer's death.

Under Balanchine the New York City Ballet developed into a living legend: a company of hand-picked dancers put through almost superhuman training to achieve a perfection that has, for nearly thirty-five years, left audiences spellbound. With 108 members, it is the biggest dance company in America; its School of American Ballet, founded by Balanchine in 1934, has more than 350 students (classes are held in the Juilliard building). The company's dancers include such names as Merrill Ashley, Suzanne Farrell, Patricia McBride, Heather Watts, Ib Andersen, Bart Cook, Sean Lavery, Adam Lüders, and Helgi Tomasson, and the active repertoire comprises no fewer than ninety pieces.

With Balanchine gone, the company has been inherited by Jerome Robbins and Peter Martins, who is also chairman of the faculty of the school. It's too soon to say just where the new direction will lead, but already there has been an infusion of a wider spectrum of contemporary styles from outside the company. Beyond question, however, the

Erie Mills and David Eisler star in the City Opera's 1982 production of Bernstein's Candide.

William Chapman and Catherine Malfitano play father and daughter in Weill's Street Scene.

Balanchine imprint will remain, a volcanic force throughout ballet. Just to be in the State Theater, for which Balanchine designed practically the entire performance area, is to be in his presence.

The Vivian Beaumont Theater and the New York Public Library at Lincoln Center—In a sense, the Repertory Theater of Lincoln Center was already in business when the Vivian Beaumont opened its doors. Elia Kazan and Robert Whitehead had booked their company to start in the winter of 1963/64 in Washington Square. By the time the Repertory Theater moved into its new quarters, it was under a second pair of directors: Jules Irving and Herbert Blau. On October 21, 1965, the theater was dedicated with Georg Büchner's *Danton's Death*. The play did badly; only the theater, with its arena seating and its thrust stage, was praised.

There should have been no trouble in luring world-class theatrical talent to work with such autonomy in such premises, but it hasn't happened, at least not yet. Blau left to help start a progressive arts school in California; Irving ran the theater alone for a few years, with some distinguished productions to his credit but nothing to permanently light up the sky. In 1973 control of the theater passed to Joseph Papp, whose downtown New York Shakespeare Festival was in microcosm what the sponsors of the Beaumont probably had in mind. Papp began bravely, with a program of plays by living American writers, including major playwrights whose first chances had come with Papp downtown. He tried everything: more new American works and classics. He brought in the iconoclastic director Andrei Serban.

In 1977, with the Vivian Beaumont and Mitzi E. Newhouse theaters open for twelve years and New York audiences still apparently dubious that "repertory" was what the city needed, Papp resigned. The house remained dark for a time and was then reopened in 1980 by the Lincoln Center Theater Company under Richmond Crinkley, with a directorate that included such names as Boston's Sarah Caldwell and Woody Allen. A dispute between Lincoln Center's board of directors and Crinkley's organization resulted in Lincoln Center's name and funds being temporarily withheld from activities at the theater. This dispute was resolved in June 1984. Meanwhile, the lights did go on, quite brilliantly, for a six-month run in 1983/84 of British director Peter Brook's remarkably effective streamlined version of Bizet's *Carmen*.

Belowstairs at the Beaumont, the tidy Off-Broadway-

Leonie Rysanek plays Elisabeth and Simon Estes is the Landgraf in a recent Metropolitan Opera production of Tannhäuser.

size Mitzi E. Newhouse Theater has also had its moments of
light and darkness. It purpose was, naturally, to accommodate experimental and showcase productions, and in its early
years a fine Monday-night series of workshops extended the
horizons of the small, enthusiastic audiences that found their
way there. Later the Newhouse was home to a brief Metropolitan Opera experiment in chamber opera, the "Mini-Met,"
which produced a repertory ranging from delightful baroque
operas to such modern fare as Virgil Thomson's famous *Four
Saints in Three Acts* before succumbing to funding problems.

Sharing the building with the Beaumont is another
small showplace—one which, however, is usually packed
—the Bruno Walter Auditorium of the New York Public
Library. Another Off-Broadway-size house, this is the scene
for many of New York's upcoming recitalists and chamber
groups, who perform free-ticket concerts every afternoon except Sunday, when the library is closed. Of course the Walter Auditorium—named after the beloved conductor—is only
part of Lincoln Center's distinguished Library & Museum
of the Performing Arts, which, bringing together the cream
of the New York Public Library's research facilities in the
arts, is one of the greatest libraries of its kind anywhere.

The library, which contains some 143,000 circulating
books and 33,500 recordings, actually consists of two dis-
tinct facilities so closely functioning that you can hardly
notice the distinction. One is the General Library and
Museum, with the open lending collection; the other is the
Performing Arts Research Center, with the serious scholar-
ly collections. Since both were designed for the use of special-
ists and laymen alike, they exist together as one unified institution. However, the third floor of the library holds most of
the research materials in music, dance, and theater, including the stunning Rodgers and Hammerstein Archives of Recorded Sound. The first two floors comprise vast stretches of
material (including records) that may be borrowed by anyone with a New York Public Library card; listening facilities;
and the children's library and story-telling area.

The Metropolitan Opera House—The largest and most expensive of Lincoln Center's palaces had to open with something
grand and bold, something new if not too new, something
that would signal to the world that the art of opera persists,
something that would also make a statement about the Metropolitan as the American eminence on the international
operatic scene. And so Samuel Barber created his grand opera
Antony and Cleopatra, to a libretto by the great iconoclast

*Renata Scotto, in the title role, clutches
Placido Domingo, as the Chevalier des
Grieux, in the Met's* Manon Lescaut.

of world theater, Franco Zeffirelli, with designs and direction also by Zeffirelli, and with a cast headed by America's Leontyne Price, then as now the pride of a great company. On September 16, 1966, it all happened, and the new $50-million house was generally well liked. Wallace Harrison had been careful to keep longtime patrons happy; his up-to-date house preserved not only the general shape but even the seat-numbering of the old house. The acoustics were judged a brilliant success; what sighs of relief there were! And if there were still a few "limited view" seats in the new house, there were far fewer than there had been at the old. Giving up the "yellow-brick brewery" wasn't easy. At a last-night gala on Thirty-ninth Street, the venerable conductor Leopold Stokowski made a futile plea from his podium to save the beautiful if useless building.

Barber's new opera was not to everyone's liking; its music was found several degrees cooler than the hot passions of the plot. Zeffirelli's staging was clearly designed to show off everything the Met's lighting board and movable-stage facilities could do, but some of his grandest effects were thwarted when, at one of the last rehearsals, a stage turntable broke down; it hadn't been designed to carry the weight of a large chorus, soloists, and a couple of camels.

If *Antony* was a mixed success on opening night, Rudolf Bing still had up his sleeve the ingredients for a terrific opening season: Marvin David Levy's *Mourning Becomes Electra*, a *Magic Flute* designed by nobody less than Marc Chagall, a Cecil Beaton-designed *Traviata*, a Beni Montresor *Gioconda*, and the first Met production ever of Richard Strauss's exotic, expressionistic fairytale *Die Frau ohne Schatten*, with extravagant and wholly wonderful sets by one of the Met's in-house designers, Robert O'Hearn.

Rudolf Bing continued at the helm of the Met until 1972, his regime marked by some dissension but also by a succession of brilliances. Placido Domingo, nurtured by the company across the way, made his Met debut during Bing's Lincoln Center years; so did Luciano Pavarotti, Marilyn Horne, Beverly Sills, and a young conductor named James Levine. A brilliant restaging of Wagner's mighty *Ring of the Nibelung* was started with the legendary Herbert von Karajan as conductor and director; he later resigned, leaving assistants to do his work. Following Bing's retirement, the chains of office went to a young Swedish director named Goeran Gentele, who charmed everyone and announced several seasons of brave, exciting plans. But Gentele was killed

James Levine (above), music director of the Metropolitan Opera, is one of the most accomplished and respected conductors on the international scene. In 1986 he will accede to the title of artistic director.

The great stage designer Jean-Pierre Ponnelle created the sets for the Met's new production of Idomeneo *(above), in 1983. The first in a projected series of Ponnelle-designed Mozart operas, it was to be followed by* La Clemenza di Tito *in 1984.*

in a car crash only weeks after joining the Met, and it befell his successor, Schuyler Chapin, to see his major projects through. These included a first Met staging of Hector Berlioz's mighty *The Trojans*, a brilliant success at its 1973 première and an equal success in its revival to begin the Met's centennial season, 1983/84.

Chapin's regime was bolstered by the appointment of the British director John Dexter to supervise theatrical aspects of Met productions; Rafael Kubelik was designated music director, but he soon left, to be replaced eventually by the growing, extraordinarily versatile James Levine. Chapin's regime lasted into 1974; his responsibilities were then assumed by Anthony Bliss, a longtime member of the Met's board of directors who is planning to retire in 1985.

Under Bliss's benevolent eye, Levine and Dexter have together built a style that maintains the Metropolitan Opera in the forefront of international houses. Levine has become one of the most important faces on the international operatic scene and is also accomplished and respected as a pianist and a conductor of symphonic works. Under his baton, the Met has achieved a more consistently cohesive sound than it had in years. In 1986 he will become artistic director of the Metropolitan Opera.

The world is not overendowed with magnetic operatic singers nowadays, and the few that there are can usually make better nightly salaries in the government-subsidized European houses. Realizing this, the Met has thrown uncommon emphasis on operas that can benefit from a theatrical approach, such as Zeffirelli's recent *La Bohème*, with its breathtaking scenic sweeps of wintertime Paris. The services of great theater designers and directors such as Zeffirelli, Otto Schenk, and Jean-Pierre Ponnelle have been enlisted with often stunning results. Among the Met's greatest triumphs in the Bliss, Levine, and Dexter era have been works that traditionally might have frightened off conservative opera-goers but don't any more—Francis Poulenc's overpowering lyric drama *Dialogues of the Carmelites*, Benjamin Britten's *Billy Budd*, and such sardonic masterpieces as Kurt Weill's *Rise and Fall of the City of Mahagonny* and Alban Berg's *Lulu*. These challenging works have placed the Metropolitan Opera in the vanguard of theatrical creativity.

The Metropolitan Opera has long been cherished by opera buffs everywhere whose only connection with live performance was through its radio broadcasts every Saturday afternoon; lately, the company has been expanding more and more into television. As of 1984, there had been thirty telecasts of "Live From the Met" performances, and five more were scheduled for the 1984/85 season. These are produced by the Metropolitan Opera Association independent of "Live From Lincoln Center" (which Lincoln Center, Inc., produces). The Met is now preparing to venture further into electronic media with the video releases of "Live From the Met" productions—so in the future when you buy a recording of a Met opera, you'll be able to see the spectacle as well as hear it.

The Metropolitan Opera gives fifty-six performances a year on the road—more than one-fifth of its season. To achieve this, the company packs off 350 performers, 1,200 costumes, 800 pairs of shoes, and 150 tons of equipment including sets, instruments, scores, wigs, props, and lights, in thirty trailer trucks and two chartered 727's. And each summer eight operas are performed in city parks to audiences that sometimes exceed 150,000. At home, on the giant Lincoln Center stage, the company gives an unmatched 210 full-blown performances of twenty-one different operas each year.

Leonard Bernstein (above), laureate conductor of the Philharmonic, leads a rehearsal with the Juilliard Orchestra.

Chicago Symphony music director Georg Solti conducts the Juilliard Orchestra.

ON CAMPUS AT LINCOLN CENTER

The Juilliard School (opposite) enjoys a vital relationship with the rest of Lincoln Center, as illustrated by two programs that bring to the school some of the great artists who pass through the Center. One program is Visiting Artists, an ongoing series of master classes begun in 1971; the other is Young Conductors, which allows top students to train with some of the world's greatest orchestra leaders.

David Ogden Stiers and Patti LuPone (opposite), then students in Juilliard's Drama Division, appear in a 1972 performance of The School for Scandal.

Luciano Pavarotti (right) leads a master class in the interpretation of Italian opera arias at Juilliard in January 1979.

The Juilliard Dance Ensemble presents There Is a Time *(below), choreographed by José Limón.*

The artistic level the company maintains through all this was reflected by the array of talent that came out for the Met's centennial gala, on October 22, 1983, the exact 100th anniversary of the Met's opening back at Thirty-ninth and Broadway. For four afternoon hours and an even longer evening session, every available Met singer from the present and recent past appeared in a dazzling procession of arias and whole scenes carried to the world on television. What made this Met centennial important was the number of younger singers, people in the bit parts at today's Met but the likely stars of tomorrow, who came on in selections of their own. There's no likelihood that the Met, the world capital of great singing, will ever run out of talent.

The Juilliard Building—With the completion of the Metropolitan Opera House and the opening two years later of Damrosch Park, the blueprint for the original Lincoln Center site had been realized. Another building remained, however, in the lot across Sixty-fifth Street. The bulk of that building holds the Juilliard School, America's most famous conservatory, its fame endowed with new luster by the recent victories of its graduates in music contests everywhere—more than 80 percent of all American winners of international music competitions were trained at Juilliard.

The school was founded in 1905 as the Institute of Musical Art and became the Juilliard School of Music in 1926, thanks to the legacy of industrialist Augustus D. Juilliard. Until it joined Lincoln Center, in 1969, it was located uptown near Columbia University. Some 925 students are enrolled at Juilliard proper, and another 275 in the Pre-College Division. For each opening at the school, about a hundred young artists apply. They come from as far away as Bulgaria and China—there are a dozen students from the People's Republic—and are chosen solely on the basis of competitive auditions.

The move to Lincoln Center gave the school new breadth, further enhancing its exalted place among the world's great schools for performers. A Theater Center was opened under the leadership of John Houseman, and a steadily growing list of its graduates have become leading actors on stage, screen, and television; its first graduating class formed the Acting Company, an independent, professional troupe that still exists today. Juilliard's American Opera Center had its debut in 1970. It trains students in all aspects of opera production and has presented nearly forty operas, including five world premières and five American premières.

In 1979 the library displayed "The Art of the Mup

The Library & Museum opened in 1965 with the evocative exhibit "Memorable Moments" (right), documenting 250 years of performance in New York.

LIBRARY AT THE CENTER

Lincoln Center's Library & Museum of the Performing Arts, a branch of the New York Public Library, combines an extensive circulating collection of books, records, and sheet music with one of the world's greatest performing-arts libraries; it also contains exhibition space, a children's library, and a recital hall.

Past sounds are preserved in the Rodgers and Hammerstein Archives.

Juilliard's Dance Division, which was founded in 1951, has prepared dancers who can be seen as solo artists all over the world. It has presented nearly thirty world premières since coming to Lincoln Center.

Four concert halls inhabit the eight-story building; of them, three are strictly associated with the school, and in them Juilliard students present 300 free concerts a year. Paul Hall is designed specifically for recitals; the Drama Theater provides full theatrical facilities and seats 206; the charming Juilliard Theater, with 1,026 seats, serves as a showcase for operas, concerts, dance, and drama. But the Juilliard building's true gleam for the concert-goer is connected only geographically to Juilliard itself. It is Alice Tully Hall, the smallest and most nearly perfect of all Lincoln Center's public halls. Alice Tully, a life-long passionate devotee of chamber music, first contributed funds for the hall and then suggested a leader and organizer for its resident chamber music ensemble: Charles Wadsworth, a well-known pianist who for several years had organized and introduced the popular chamber concerts at Gian Carlo Menotti's Festival of Two Worlds, in the Italian hill town of Spoleto.

A sense of quiet absorption prevails at the reading tables on the library's main floor. Students, scholars, and professionals come from all over to use the research facilities; others come just to browse and borrow.

The result was a group that not only raised the standards of chamber music concert-planning the country over, but also attracted audiences so varied that the whole idea of chamber music's being for a stuffy few was completely shattered. Rather than restricting the Chamber Music Society of Lincoln Center to the customary string quartet, Wadsworth assembled an assortment that cut across many fields: wind players, strings, brass, a singer, and guest artists, all first-rate players giving up several months a year of concert performance to come and play together.

A typically adventurous program, performed for packed houses in the winter of 1983/84, included a Handel cantata and some Mahler songs sung by Frederica von Stade, a superb young American mezzo-soprano, with Wadsworth at the harpsichord for the Handel. Then there was a rare performance of the original version, for chamber ensemble, of Aaron Copland's *Appalachian Spring*. At the end, eight string players combined forces in Mendelssohn's lively, youthful Octet. As chamber programs go, one like this seems uncommonly wide-ranging, but that has been the Chamber Music Society's premise since its start. The Society's concerts come close to selling out, both at home and on tour: more than any single group, Wadsworth's ensemble has sparked a major chamber music revival among listeners of all ages, and chamber music audiences all over the country have become much larger and more avid than ever before. The Society has even created a novel series of experimental workshops for seventh- to twelfth-grade students and their teachers. These bear the title "Together with Chamber Music" and provide educational experiences to invited audiences from public and parochial schools both in the city and up to fifty miles away.

Like the Chamber Music Society and Mostly Mozart, the Film Society of Lincoln Center is one of the Center's own creations. Film became part of Lincoln Center in 1963 when the first annual New York Film Festival was held. By 1967 the beginning of the Film Society of Lincoln Center was in view. Since then a staggering repertory of motion pictures—foreign and American—has been introduced to capacity audiences. Such directors as France's Jean-Luc Godard, whose cynical romances at early festivals placed his name indelibly before the public, or the American Martin Scorsese, whose *Mean Streets* was a festival hit, owe much of their reputation to early exposure at the festival. Also, each spring the Film Society gives, in conjunction with the Museum of Modern Art, a New Directors/New Films festival, introducing dozens more new movies from around the world. And in recent years the Society has expanded its activities to include a series of "homages" to the great living men and women of cinema. In 1972, Charles Chaplin, one of the greatest figures in the history of film, was lured back to the land of his greatest triumphs for a personal tribute. Similarly honored have been Fred Astaire, Joanne Woodward and Paul Newman, George Cukor, Bob Hope, John Huston, Billy Wilder, Claudette Colbert, Alfred Hitchcock, Barbara Stanwyck, and Laurence Olivier.

Forty years ago it might have been unthinkable to associate symphony, opera, ballet, and theater with an art as populace-oriented as film. However, the presence of film at Lincoln Center reflects a recognition of the medium's importance in today's culture. Each year's New York Film Festival usually includes one or two forgotten masterpieces but also gives premières of important new films—*Chariots of Fire* and *The Night of the Shooting Stars* are recent examples—and maintains an awareness of the importance of film to younger audiences. Tastemaker? Or merely an uncommonly keen observer of taste? Very likely Lincoln Center, acting on its own artistic conscience or invoking the collective conscience of its constituents, is a little of both.

6
Lincoln Center, U.S.A.

As Lincoln Center was taking shape, the arts leadership of the world watched and wondered. New York's leadership had its initial doubts about the wisdom of lumping so much culture together; the annals are full of statements—as late as in 1962 by the New York City Opera's Julius Rudel, for instance—that Lincoln Center couldn't, wouldn't work, that the centralization of so many segments of New York's musical life would rob each segment of its personality.

Rudel needn't have worried; he certainly didn't seem worried when, four years later, his own company had its triumphant Lincoln Center opening. Here was Lincoln Center, with its own sphere of activity; there was the City Opera, with its. Never need, or should, the twain meet. What made the arts-center concept work, above all, was the enormously heightened visibility it bestowed upon its constituents. New York had always had its legendary musical shrines: Carnegie Hall, Town Hall, the old Metropolitan Opera—these were entries in any tourist's itinerary. As buildings, however, they weren't all that imposing.

The Alkuone Dance Company of Belgium kicks off the Lincoln Center Out-of-Doors season in August 1978. With more than sixty events in the open air, Lincoln Center becomes the site of a month-long free festival each summer.

Above, New Yorkers of all ages enjoy Lincoln Center's outdoor fare. The August events began in 1971 as the Lincoln Center Community/Street Theater Festival and became known as Lincoln Center Out-of-Doors three years later.

The great triumph of grouping New York's cultural facilities on one piece of real estate was that Lincoln Center itself became a place to see, to visit. A concert or opera is still a major "must" for the New Yorker and the visitor, but so is a guided tour of Lincoln Center itself, a series of looks backstage at the great houses, conveying the wonder that vibrates through every square inch of this remarkable planned space for the arts, indoors and outdoors as well.

The fears of some New Yorkers that the centralization of the city's musical life would snuff out smaller arts enclaves around town have been dispelled. In fact, the visible presence of Lincoln Center has helped feed a growing arts appetite that one set of buildings cannot begin to satisfy. It stretches no point to look at Lincoln Center as the catalyst that has made possible the great resurgence of concert activity across town at the YMHA at Ninety-second Street and Lexington Avenue, at the Grace Rainey Rogers Auditorium and other spaces at the Metropolitan Museum, and, above all, at the Brooklyn Academy of Music, in which a complex of performing spaces large and small has become a kind of Lincoln-Center-under-one-roof, with imaginative programming slanted toward the avant-garde that in no way competes with the Manhattan prototype.

Across the nation, cultural leaders have taken to heart the lesson of how the arts benefit from the big architectural concept and the heightened visibility it engenders. Nowhere can the impact of the Lincoln Center idea be better measured than in Los Angeles. There, in the fall of 1964, the formidable Dorothy Chandler, whose husband ran the city's

biggest newspaper, welcomed the Los Angeles citizenry to a Music Center that was largely her own doing: three grand buildings for the arts. It was a daring move, all the more so since Los Angeles had never boasted the commitment to the serious arts that had always motivated New York. Now the Music Center has helped create that commitment.

Washington, D.C., needed something along the lines of Lincoln Center as an arts center worthy of the nation's capital. President John F. Kennedy envisioned such a project; with realities of congressional funding, it wasn't until two presidents later, on a muggy September night in 1971, that the John F. Kennedy Center for the Performing Arts held its gala opening.

At Lincoln Center—or at the Music Center in Los Angeles or at the Kennedy Center—there is an ongoing interplay, difficult to grasp but fascinating to consider, between the creative impulses of the individual components of an arts complex and those of the center itself. In Lincoln Center's early days there was plenty of controversy as to who was running what: William Schuman attempting to plan seasons at the Vivian Beaumont, Rudolf Bing kicking up a fuss over the New York City Opera's "encroachment." The cultural corridors of Los Angeles and Washington have been clouded by similar dustups. It is in the nature of the artistic beast, after all, for feelings to run high and strong.

Yet there are positive aspects to the interplay of component and central leadership that far outweigh any conflict. The central leadership is itself nearly invisible at Lincoln Center, yet its work is felt by all who visit the complex, and

Above, the Dayton Contemporary Dance Company from Dayton, Ohio, performs in the Guggenheim Bandshell. INSET: *the Multigravitational Aerodance Group flies through the air beside Avery Fisher Hall.*

it provides a wide range of valuable programs and services that would be unavailable to the constituents were they left entirely on their own. "People think we're just a landlord," says Martin E. Segal, chairman of Lincoln Center for the Performing Arts, Inc. "But basically our job is to attempt to do for each constituent whatever it can't do for itself, or what a central organization can do better for all. For example, we raise money from the corporate sector to help with the operating expenses of each of the constituents, making a single appeal for all. We conduct most of the programs for the community, including Lincoln Center Out-of-Doors and the Community Holiday Festival, and we give the Lincoln Center tours. We run Mostly Mozart, introducing a series of musical events in the summertime. We are in charge of the Great Performers series, highlighting fine artists in all the art forms. We deal with the federal, state, and local governments. We maintain a liaison with other arts activities elsewhere in the city and the country. We conduct the Lincoln Center Institute, because it is clearly important to have an educational effort that supplements the richly varied offerings of all the constituents at once, with aesthetic-education programs for teachers and students. And we do all these things because they are more efficiently done centrally. Of course, we are also the landlord—we care about and pay attention to the buildings and the grounds."

Segal has been chairman of Lincoln Center, Inc., since 1981. He is just the third person to have held that position, following John D. Rockefeller 3rd, the founding father, and Amyas Ames, who succeeded Rockefeller in 1970. William Schuman, the first president of Lincoln Center, served until the end of 1968; he was followed, after an interval, by John W. Mazzola, who served until 1982. The current president, former New York City Deputy Mayor for Operations Nathan Leventhal, took office in March 1984.

When Ames took the helm, he was already chairman of the Philharmonic's board and had been deeply involved in helping settle Lincoln Center's financial problems. It was under his leadership that Lincoln Center began its annual Out-of-Doors festival, in 1971, and the Lincoln Center Institute emerged in its present form. The redesign and rebuilding of Avery Fisher Hall occurred during his tenure, in 1976. "Live From Lincoln Center" telecasts also began in 1976, and the series has expanded rapidly ever since.

LIVE IN YOUR LIVING ROOM

An estimated 100 million Americans have seen and heard Lincoln Center performances on television since "Live From Lincoln Center" began in 1976. Low-light camera technology had to be specially developed for the series, which has won many awards, including five Emmys and two Grammys.

An almost-hidden camera pans the audience as a performer takes a curtain call during a pioneering cable broadcast of the City Opera's Le Coq D'Or *in 1971.*

A technician adjusts one of eight camera positions as Philharmonic members rehearse prior to a live telecast.

Leontyne Price sings and Zubin Mehta conducts during a gala benefit concert opening the Philharmonic's fall 1982 season, aired live nationwide over public-broadcasting TV stations.

At right is the scene in the control room during the concert shown above. A technical and creative staff of almost fifty works on each production for "Live From Lincoln Center."

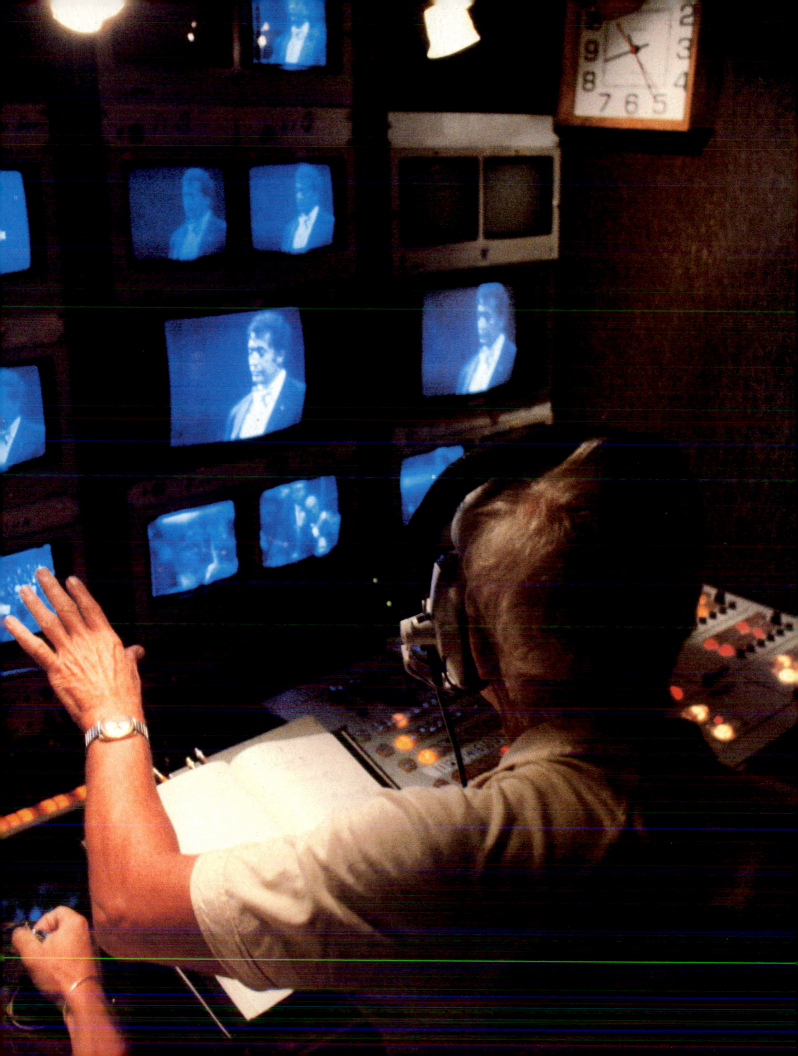

Luciano Pavarotti accepts applause after a live telecast with the Philharmonic.

Danny Kaye and Zubin Mehta complete a "Live" performa[

Pia Lindstrom (left) interviews ballerina Natalia Makarova for the intermission segment of a "Live" telecast.

Nowhere does the benevolence of consolidated arts-center leadership cast a brighter and broader glow than on those "Live From Lincoln Center" nights on Public Broadcasting, right on your television screen. From the beginning of the center's planning, it was hoped that TV would play a major role in the future of the arts in America. With producer John Goberman in charge, there remained only to determine what sort of fare would make the monster happy.

It's not a simple problem. There's a vast difference between what might look good to an audience in a concert hall or opera house and what looks good to a television camera. There's another huge difference between what seems like a cultural event to a live audience and what can suggest the quality of that event to a viewing audience at home. It might be enthralling to sit for two hours in Avery Fisher Hall watching Zubin Mehta conduct the orchestra, but an audience that grew up on *Gunsmoke* can be pardoned for wanting a little more action.

Young dancers from the School of American Ballet marvel at the TV equipment before a performance of Coppelia.

Conductor David Zinman leads an outdoor rehearsal of the Mostly Mozart Festival Orchestra.

But where is the action? Let's watch a few moments of "Live From Lincoln Center" and find out. Here is Mehta, leading the New York Philharmonic through Igor Stravinsky's seventy-one-year-old-but-still-shocking *Rite of Spring.* Here is an incredible passage for the strings, wildly stomping and syncopated; there, on the screen, are the Philharmonic strings digging ferociously into the passage; there are Mehta's eyes, transfixed by the daring in Stravinsky's score that remains so vivid through the years. Now comes the harrowing tuba solo that brings the first part to a close, and there on the screen is the Philharmonic's tuba player: how can any single human, we ask, draw so dramatic a sound from that ugly mess of brass plumbing! As the camera focuses on one scene of high activity after another, we almost get the feeling that some highly artistic, superbly dramatized version of the printed score is there on the screen, lending an extraordinary new dimension to the music.

Let's try another one: Luciano Pavarotti in recital, one of the events in Lincoln Center's "Great Performers" series, televised live from Avery Fisher Hall. What's to look at with a portly man singing songs and a bookish type at the piano? Watch and learn. From out front in the hall we

wonder at the ease of Pavarotti at work, the way he encompasses those gorgeous *bel canto* phrases seemingly without flicking a muscle. But watch the screen; observe close up how a great artist can cloak strenuous effort with the trappings of ease; watch the perspiration roll like gumdrops as Pavarotti glides effortlessly from one song to the next. Observe the rest of the man. Every singer who perspires, every singer with fillings in his molars and caps up front, can stand a little taller from the sight of Pavarotti's humanness close up.

Shall we try another? Televising opera can be a real problem; wonderfully subtle stage lighting that looks beautiful in the house can reach the camera as black-on-black; yet an audience that buys tickets for a night at the New York City Opera doesn't want its opera tampered with for the sake of the media. Producer Goberman worked long and hard to find television equipment sensitive enough to work with available light, and the beauty of the City Opera on television proves the success of his efforts. Better yet, the equipment in the hall itself works so quietly that only the nosiest spectator is aware that a huge TV camera may be at work right at his elbow.

The Westminster Choir, performing with the Festival Orchestra and conductor Robert Shaw, appears at the Mostly Mozart Festival in August 1982.

Intelligently produced, a televised opera can be a dazzling experience. Enormous amounts of time are spent at rehearsals, trying to second-guess what part of the action would naturally hold the viewer's attention at any given time. Maybe we don't *want* to be up there on the stage as chubby Edgardo makes love to a Lucia twice his height, or as Manon bids farewell to a table that is obviously a bit of knocked-together plywood. But then the camera pulls back, and the magic of a whole stage full of music takes over. And at intermission we are escorted backstage, a privilege we'd never enjoy at a live performance. Now we can *really* get to the heart of the matter: a bright young singer in Renaissance costume clutching a can of Coca-Cola; impresario Beverly Sills wandering through the chaos offering encouragement. As hardened a TV veteran as anyone in opera, Sills, stops by for a chat. Did it bother her when she sang on that stage with microphones and cameras nearby? "Not at all," the soprano replied. "I was so astigmatic that I couldn't see them anyway."

It is estimated that "Live From Lincoln Center" broadcasts have reached American households more than 209 million times. They have received twenty-three Emmy nominations, five Emmy awards, two Grammys, the George Foster Peabody Award, and the Television Critics Circle Award.

"Live From Lincoln Center" isn't the only activity that can't be contained by Lincoln Center's buildings. Thanks to Leonard de Paur, Lincoln Center's director of community relations, Lincoln Center Out-of-Doors offers performances in the open spaces between the buildings every summer. For three full weeks a year the festival presents music, dance, and theater events designed to appeal to people of all ages and backgrounds— all for free. Its audience totals over 200,000. In December there's an all-free festival especially for children and their families: the Community Holiday Festival. Its offerings range from opera productions for children to showcase performances by talented area youths.

Indoors, Lincoln Center, Inc., has created a sort of continual festival with the Great Performers series, which presents fifty solo recitals, chamber and orchestral performances, and jazz, pop, and folk-rock events a year in two halls, Alice

Across the street from Lincoln Center, several new buildings have gone up and another is just getting under way. The entire Upper West Side has undergone a major cultural and economic revival since Lincoln Center opened.

Tully and Avery Fisher. Great Performers began twenty years ago, conceived, according to William W. Lockwood, Jr., Lincoln Center's director of programming, "strictly as a recital series—to revive what was then believed to be the dying art of the solo recital." Today the series has grown to feature artists such as—to name a few—cellist Yo-Yo Ma, guitarist Andrés Segovia, the Guarneri Quartet; pianists Emanuel Ax, Alicia de Larrocha, Vladimir Ashkenazy, and Rudolf Serkin; the Philadelphia and Cleveland orchestras; and singers Marilyn Horne, Kathleen Battle, and Teresa Berganza. Great Performers adds a stunning assortment of entries to Lincoln Center's already copious menu.

We talk about Lincoln Center as the focus of musical life for New York, but that is only the narrow view. For the tourists who pour into the city day after day and make straightaway for Sixty-fourth and Columbus, for the hopefuls who come from everywhere on the map to audition for an opera job, a Philharmonic chair, or acceptance to Juilliard, and for the millions who learn of its artistic wonders through their television sets, Lincoln Center is a national artistic resource. It would be so even if the offices of America's music industry—managements, press agents, record companies, publishers—weren't located within a few blocks. The outreach of Lincoln Center through the media—the "Live From Lincoln Center" telecasts, the separate TV series from the Metropolitan Opera, the radio broadcasts from the Philharmonic and the Met—has created a cultural awareness throughout the country and the world that is all the assurance we require that the arts are secure in our time.

And for times to come? Let's look in on the assembly hall of an elementary school. It might be in New York City or out in the suburbs. A musical ensemble is up on the stage—a wind quintet, perhaps, or a mixed ensemble, or a group of singers. It is there because it has been sent by Lincoln Center's Student Program, which organizes a vast network of in-school concerts throughout the Northeast. The performers finish; the kids in the audience draw closer and ask questions. How do you take your clarinet apart? Why do you keep turning your horn upside down? Where did you learn to sing Italian? When are you coming back? Here is the next generation of Lincoln Center's audience, tomorrow's record buyers, TV watchers, Philharmonic first-desk players, operatic prima donnas, and they are learning what there is in the musical world. Not every one of them will grow up a dedicated connoisseur of the arts, but every one of them has the chance now to decide such things for himself.

Each of Lincoln Center's constituents has its own edu-

LINCOLN CENTER GOES TO SCHOOLS

The Lincoln Center Institute provides a strong link between the Center and area schools. As many as 600 teachers from New York, New Jersey, and Connecticut attend Institute workshops each July to explore new ways of teaching the arts. As a result, some 80,000 students attend live performances that the Institute presents.

At an Institute summer session for teachers, choreographer Antony Tudor demonstrates the power of gesture.

Aaron Copland conducts his Appalachian Spring for the benefit of teachers at a 1979 Institute summer session.

Teachers use percussion instruments to perform a musical score that they created in an Institute summer workshop.

Right, dancer Schellie Archbold directs a movement workshop for schoolteachers; below, two Juilliard artists explore a musical work with a junior high school class. The Lincoln Center Institute has proved so successful that it has become the model for similar educational programs in seven states.

cational program, and to enhance their several ventures in educational outreach, the Lincoln Center Institute was established in 1974. The idea for it was first developed in 1971, when Mark Schubart, now director of the Lincoln Center Institute, took a year off with a Carnegie Foundation grant to study arts education. Explaining the Institute's purpose, Schubart has said, "Rather than teaching students how to 'appreciate' the arts, we should be focusing on how the arts can help young people discover their own capacities to make aesthetic choices in their lives and ultimately how to exercise their *right* to decide how their world is to look and sound."

At a time when municipal funds for arts education are suffering cutbacks in many cities, the Institute advises and trains public school teachers in methods of teaching arts perception to their children. Under Institute auspices, some six hundred teachers from around the country gather in New York each summer to glean expert advice on, well, survival for the arts and for the people who will enjoy the arts in the years to come. They learn to teach the arts by bringing performance to the students and by nurturing and nourishing creativity rather than by conveying preconceived notions. The concept has proved such a success that similar programs modeled on the Lincoln Center Institute have been established in five states.

Important? Yes, beyond question. The architects of Lincoln Center planned their buildings to last: not only through the strength of stone and steel and glass, but through the even greater moral strength of the arts these buildings were built to house. The persistence of the buildings is not enough, of itself, to ensure the persistence of the arts. These latter depend on the uncertain: the whims of the agencies, public and private, that pay the bills; the courage of those few adventurers who dare to create new art to ward off the stagnation of the timeworn and the over-familiar; the efforts of teachers and other communicators who do what they can to spread word of the greatness of great art to those of all ages who will listen. Lincoln Center was planned and built in the faith that these forces would continue in the world. Its planners and builders had no assurance that their faith was justified, of course, but there is no sign that their actions were ever slowed by doubts.

The words of John D. Rockefeller 3rd, at the groundbreaking of Lincoln Center back in May 1959, summed up this faith simply and succinctly: "I believe it is important for our city. I believe it is important for our country. I believe it is important for the world."

Martin E. Segal (in front), chairman of the board of Lincoln Center for the Performing Arts, Inc., and Nathan Leventhal, president, pose in the plaza of Lincoln Center.

PICTURE CREDITS

LINCOLN CENTER

Metropolitan Opera House

The New York Public Library
at Lincoln Center

Vivian Beaumont
Theater

Mitzi E. Newhouse
Theater

Center Concourse

The Center At
Lincoln Center

New York State Theater

South Concourse

North Concourse

The Juilliard School

Avery Fisher Hall

Alice Tully Hall

East Concourse

Concourse Level

Lincoln Center Drive South

Lincoln Center Drive North

West 62nd Street

West 65th Street

West 66th Street

Amsterdam Avenue

Columbus Avenue

Broadway

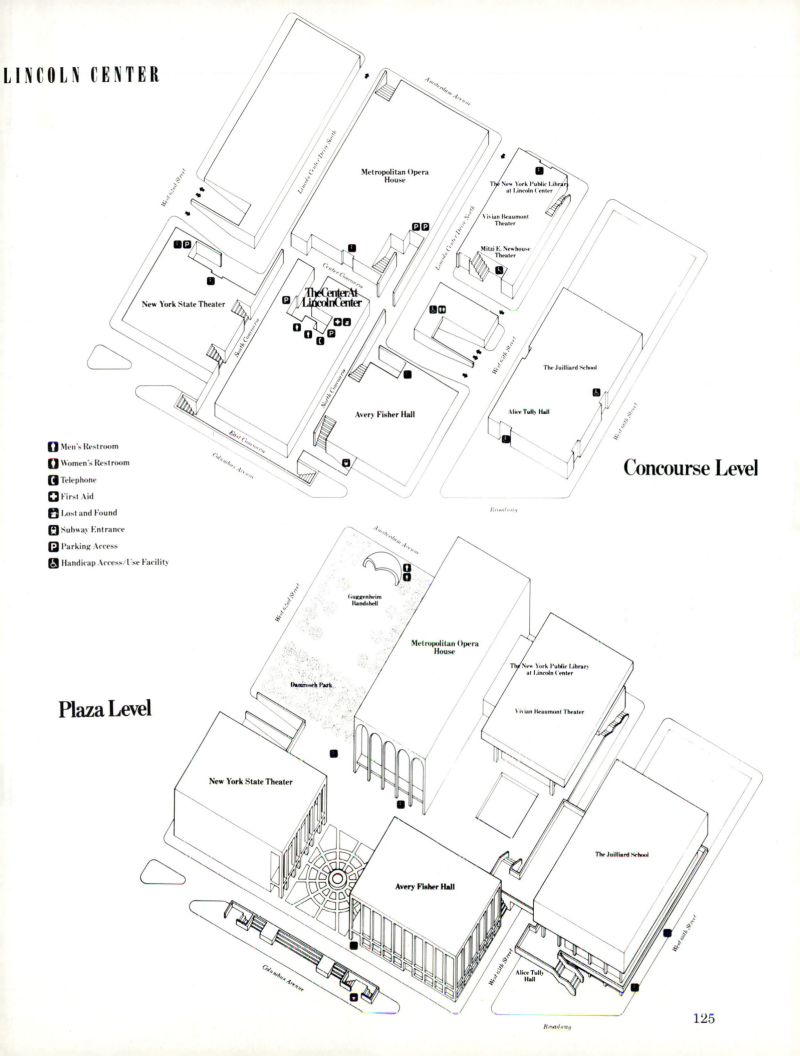

- 🚹 Men's Restroom
- 🚺 Women's Restroom
- ☎ Telephone
- ✚ First Aid
- Lost and Found
- Subway Entrance
- P Parking Access
- ♿ Handicap Access/Use Facility

Plaza Level

Guggenheim
Bandshell

Metropolitan Opera
House

The New York Public Library
at Lincoln Center

Vivian Beaumont Theater

Damrosch Park

New York State Theater

The Juilliard School

Avery Fisher Hall

Alice Tully
Hall

Amsterdam Avenue

West 62nd Street

West 65th Street

West 66th Street

Columbus Avenue

Broadway

Lincoln Center for the Performing Arts, Inc.

ADMINISTRATION

Leonard de Paur, Director, Community Relations
William W. Lockwood, Jr., Executive Producer, Programming
John Goberman, Executive Producer, Television
Mark Schubart, Director, Lincoln Center Institute
Richard Baker, Associate Director, Media Development
Robert Crane, Associate Director, Lincoln Center Institute
June Dunbar, Associate Director, Lincoln Center Institute
Delmar D. Hendricks, Booking Director, Concert Halls
Hattie K. Jutagir, Associate Director, Development
Joe McKaughan, Associate Director, Public Information
David Oldham, Director, Operations and Central Facility
   Services
Robert Ronan, Director, Personnel
Theresa R. Schaff, Associate Director, Development
Susanne Faulkner Stevens, Associate Director, Public
   Information
Robert Turner, General Manager, Concert Halls

THE LINCOLN CENTER COUNCIL

Anthony A. Bliss, Metropolitan Opera
Richmond Crinkley, Vivian Beaumont Theater, Inc.
Dr. Vartan Gregorian, The New York Public Library
Lincoln Kirstein, New York City Ballet
Joanne Koch, The Film Society of Lincoln Center
Nathan Leventhal, Lincoln Center
Martin J. Oppenheimer, City Center of Music and Drama
Mark Schubart, Lincoln Center Institute
Beverly Sills, New York City Opera
Charles Wadsworth, Chamber Music Society of Lincoln
   Center
Gideon Waldrop, The Juilliard School
Albert K. Webster, New York Philharmonic

LINCOLN CENTER COUNCIL ON
EDUCATIONAL PROGRAMS

Mark Schubart, Lincoln Center Institute (Chairman)
Joanne Cossa, Chamber Music Society of Lincoln Center
JoAnn Forman, Metropolitan Opera and Metropolitan
   Opera Guild
Edwin S. Holmgren, New York Public Library
Nancy Kelly, New York City Opera
Wendy Keys, The Film Society of Lincoln Center
Mrs. Norman Lassalle, New York City Ballet
Mary H. Smith, The Juilliard School
Daniel Windham, New York Philharmonic

Lincoln Center Facts

AVERY FISHER HALL

Home of: New York Philharmonic
Opening date: September 23, 1962
Architect: Max Abramovitz of Harrison & Abramovitz
Renamed Avery Fisher Hall: September 20, 1973
Auditorium demolished and rebuilt: May 15–October, 1976
Opening date of new auditorium: October 19, 1976
Acoustical consultant: Dr. Cyril M. Harris
Architects: Philip Johnson and John Burgee of Johnson/Burgee
Seating capacity: 2,742

LINCOLN CENTER PLAZA

Opening date: April 6, 1964
Architects: Fountain—Philip Johnson
            Concourse and Reflecting Pool—Harrison &
               Abramovitz
Renovations of plaza surfaces: May, 1982–February, 1983
Architects: Philip Johnson and John Burgee of Johnson/
            Burgee
Financing: The public areas, including the Plaza and

Damrosch Park, are owned by the City of New York and reconstructed with capital funds provided by the City of New York with the cooperation of the Department of Cultural Affairs.

NEW YORK STATE THEATER

Home of: New York City Ballet
         New York City Opera
Opening date: April 23, 1964
Architect: Philip Johnson
Acoustical reconstruction: July 5–August 24, 1982
Opening date of reconstructed auditorium: September 7,
   1982
Acoustical consultant: Dr. Cyril M. Harris
Architects: Philip Johnson and John Burgee of Johnson/
            Burgee
Financing: Fan Fox and Leslie R. Samuels Foundation
           City of New York
           Helen Huntington Hull Fund
Seating capacity: 2,792

VIVIAN BEAUMONT THEATER and
MITZI E. NEWHOUSE THEATER

Home of: Lincoln Center Theater Company
Opening date: October 21, 1965
Architect: Eero Saarinen & Associates
Collaborating designer: Jo Mielziner
Seating capacity: Vivian Beaumont Theater—1,000–1,089
                  Mitzi E. Newhouse Theater—280

THE NEW YORK PUBLIC LIBRARY
AT LINCOLN CENTER

Home of : General Library and Museum of the Performing
          Arts Performing Arts Research Center
Opening date: November 30,1965
Architects: Skidmore, Owings & Merrill
Seating capacity: Bruno Walter Auditorium—212
                  The Heckscher Oval—80

METROPOLITAN OPERA HOUSE

Home of: Metropolitan Opera
Opening date: September 16,1966
Architect: Wallace K. Harrison of Harrison & Abramovitz
Seating capacity: Auditorium—3,788 (standing room—200)
                  List Hall—144

GUGGENHEIM BANDSHELL—DAMROSCH PARK

Under the City of New York's Department of Cultural
Affairs and Department of Recreation
Opening date: May 22, 1969
Architect: The Eggars Partnership
Seating capacity: 2,500–3,500

ALICE TULLY HALL

Home of: The Chamber Music Society of Lincoln Center
Opening date: September 11, 1969
Architect: Pietro Belluschi
Associate architects: Eduardo Catalano & Helge Wester-
                      mann
Seating capacity: 1,096

THE JUILLIARD SCHOOL

Opening date: October 26, 1969
Architect: Pietro Belluschi
Associate architects: Eduardo Catalano & Helge Wester-
                      mann
Seating capacity: The Juillard Theater 1,026
                  Paul Recital Hall 278
                  Drama Workshop 206

LINCOLN CENTER PARK & LOCK GARAGE

Architect: Harrison & Abramovitz
Parking capacity: 700

THE CENTER AT LINCOLN CENTER

Home of: The Lincoln Center Performing Arts Shop, the
Tour Desk, and Lincoln Center Gallery
Opening date: November 28, 1980

The Constituent Members of Lincoln Center

THE METROPOLITAN OPERA

William Rockefeller, *Chairman of the Board*
James S. Marcus, *Chairman of the Executive Committee*
Bruce Crawford, *President*
J. William Fisher, *Vice President*
Mrs. Alexander M. Laughlin, *Vice President*
Laurence D. Lovett, *Vice President*
Mrs. Stephen O'Neil, *Vice President*
Michael V. Forrestal, *Treasurer*
Alton E. Peters, *Secretary*

THE NEW YORK PHILHARMONIC

Amyas Ames, *Honorary Chairman*
Carlos Moseley, *Chairman*
Peter S. Heller, *Vice Chairman*
Phyllis J. Mills, *Vice Chairman*
Gurnee F. Hart, *Vice Chairman*
Mrs. Robert L. Hoguet, *President*
Albert K. Webster, *Executive Vice President*
Anthony P. Terracciano, *Treasurer*
Maynard E. Steiner, *Vice President-Finance*
J. Buckhout Johnston, *Secretary*

THE JUILLIARD SCHOOL

Peter S. Paine, *Chairman*
Ralph F. Leach, *Vice Chairman*
John J. Costello, *Secretary*

THE NEW YORK PUBLIC LIBRARY

Mrs. Vincent Astor, *Honorary Chairman of the Board of Trustees*

Andrew Heiskell, *Chairman*
Dr. Vartan Gregorian, *President and Chief Executive Officers*
Gregory R. Long, *Vice-President of Public Affairs and Development*
John H. Masten, *Vice-President for Budget, Planning, and Operations*
David H. Stamm, *Andrew W. Mellon Director of Research Libraries*
Ralph E. Hansmann, *Treasurer*
Robert R. Douglass, *Secretary*

NEW YORK CITY BALLET

Orville H. Schell, *Chairman*
Gillian Attfield, *President*
Mrs. Nathan L. Halpern, *Vice-President*
Marvin A. Asnes, *Treasurer*
Mrs. Irving Mitchell Felt, *Secretary*

NEW YORK CITY OPERA

Robert W. Wilson, *Chairman*
Martin J. Oppenheimer, *Vice-Chairman*
Lloyd Rigler, *Vice-President*
David Moxley, *Treasurer*
James C. Marlas, *Secretary*

THE FILM SOCIETY OF LINCOLN CENTER

Dorothy Cullman, *Chairman*
Saul Jeffee, *Vice-Chairman*
Julien J. Studley, *Vice-Chairman*
Alfred R. Stern, *President*
Sheldon Gunsberg, *Vice-President*
Roy L. Furman, *Treasurer*
Michael F. Mayer, *Secretary*

CHAMBER MUSIC SOCIETY OF LINCOLN CENTER

Miss Alice Tully, *Chairman*
William Schuman, *Vice-Chairman*
Henry S. Ziegler, *President*
Isaac Shapiro, *Vice-President*
Mrs. James R. Houghton, *Secretary*
Dr. John A. Cook, *Treasurer*

THE VIVIAN BEAUMONT THEATER

Mrs. Linda LeRoy Janklow, *Chairman*
Mrs. Adele G. Block, *President*
Mr. Ray Larsen, *Treasurer*
Mr. Paul Bauman, *Secretary*